WOODBURNING
with Style

WOODBURNING
with Style

by Simon Easton

FOX CHAPEL
PUBLISHING

ISBN 978-1-56523-443-7

Library of Congress Cataloging-in-Publication Data

Easton, Simon.
    Woodburning with style / by Simon Easton.
        p. cm.
    Includes index.
    ISBN 978-1-56523-443-7
    1. Pyrography. I. Title.
    TT199.8.E28 2010
    745.51--dc22
                                                2009053467

To learn more about the other great books from Fox Chapel Publishing, or to find a retailer near you, call toll-free 800-457-9112 or visit us at *www.FoxChapelPublishing.com*.

Note to Authors: We are always looking for talented authors to write new books in our area of woodworking, design, and related crafts. Please send a brief letter describing your idea to Acquisition Editor, 1970 Broad Street, East Petersburg, PA 17520.

Printed in China
First printing: April 2010

Because burning wood and other materials inherently includes the risk of injury and damage, this book cannot guarantee that creating the projects in this book is safe for everyone. For this reason, this book is sold without warranties or guarantees of any kind, expressed or implied, and the publisher and the author disclaim any liability for any injuries, losses, or damages caused in any way by the content of this book or the reader's use of the tools needed to complete the projects presented here. The publisher and the author urge all woodburners to thoroughly review each project and to understand the use of all tools before beginning any project.

About the Author

Simon Easton studied a BA (Hons) Three-Dimensional Design degree at Manchester Metropolitan University where he focused on woodturning, silversmithing, and pewterware. His pewter napkin ring set was one of the MMU winners of the Pewter Live 1999 competition, and was displayed at Pewterers' Hall in London. He won both a Precious Metals Bursary and a grant from the Worshipful Company of Goldsmiths in order to produce design concepts that he had developed. The common theme in Simon's work was a decorative and textural feel, often rich in embellishment or pattern.

Before graduating in 2000, Simon's design for a wooden turned decorative bowl was selected for inclusion in the *onetree* project. This project, which toured the United Kingdom as an exhibition, stemmed from the use of one single ailing oak tree distributed to a range of artists, designers, manufacturers, and craftspeople. Every single part of the tree (from the leaves to the roots) was used to create a stirring and diverse display of talent, which was also featured in a book published to accompany the tour. For the *onetree* exhibition, Simon created a decorative turned wooden bowl with a spun pewter insert, entitled *Wish, Hope, Dream, Everything*.

In recent years, Simon's crafting focus and love of wood has led him to the art of pyrography, which he uses with a contemporary twist to create richly decorative items and gifts. The result is a body of work released under the name *Wood Tattoos*. He has created a varied range of works and commissions, sells at craft fairs and galleries, and accepts custom orders at *www.woodtattoos.com*. He is an active member and moderator of the UK Crafts Forum, where he assists in passing on tips and advice to all craftspeople.

Dedication

This book is dedicated with my love and appreciation to the following people:

To my wife, Jane, for her continued love during the long nights in front of the computer and always.

To my daughter, Bethan, and my stepsons, Howell, Harry, and Freddie, for distracting me at every opportunity!

To my parents-in-law, Peggy & Gilbert, and my grandmother, Molly, for their unquestioning care and support.

And in loving memory of my grandfather, Ted, who helped to develop my love of the visual image. I miss you.

Contents

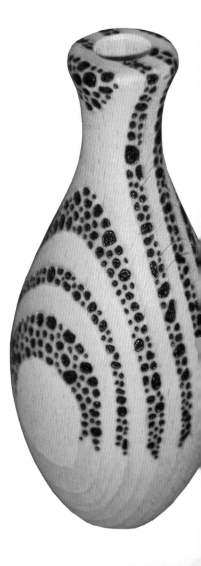

Introduction

Wood Tattoos is the name I've given to my creations using the art of pyrography. There is such visual similarity between the tattoo artist transferring inks to the skin of their client and the pyrographer burning their decorative designs into a piece of wood. I may be slightly unusual (some might say incredibly strange!), but I also find both processes extremely relaxing. The tattoos on my body all mean something to me about a certain stage in my life, and I believe that crafts such as pyrography also have the ability to create something to cherish or remember. I try to recreate that richness and meaning in my pyrography work.

As our technologies have progressed, production techniques have become more advanced and the role of the craftsperson has become more specialized or even marginalized. Handcrafted pieces appeal to us, as they have an identity that many mass-produced items lack. There is often a story behind them, something magical and intangible that can enthral us. The future for such possessions may seem uncertain in the increasingly transient modern culture. How do we form an emotional connection with an item we can only see on a computer screen? How do we experience the warmth, the texture, or the smell of such things? The tactile and sensory pleasure of life is all part of the variety that makes working in crafts so pleasurable and challenging.

Pyrography has always struck me as a community craft, as its practitioners are always so open to sharing tips and techniques. In this book, I hope to give you a feel for my *Wood Tattoos* style of pyrography, which may be both similar and wildly different than other books written on the subject. Each chapter contains a wealth of information about the techniques and methods I use to create my own designs. Pyrography is an artistic process and it would be impossible to create a definitive list of the ways it can be used, so this book is designed to show you how I have achieved the results for my own work and to start you on the path to discovering your

> This book is designed to show you how I have achieved the results for my own work and to start you on the path to discovering your own techniques and style.

own techniques and style. As with all areas of art, each individual will bring their own individual qualities, interpretations, and ways of expression to their work, making us all uniquely different. As you progress through the chapters, it is my hope your pyrography skills will build until you feel able to achieve whatever results you desire.

I have also created a number of step-by-step projects to help you try out some of the ideas and tips described: the projects are designed to act as guidance for inspiration, rather than to be followed exactly to the letter, leaving you scope to follow your own creativity. There are galleries of my work included to show you the range of potential available to you when you take up the art of woodburning. Above all else, I hope you pick up on the pleasure that working in pyrography gives me, and take some of that away to inspire your own crafting vision.

And one final word of warning before you start—don't confuse a pyrography machine with a tattoo kit. It would hurt!

Getting Started will fill you in on what you need to know before you start burning. Page 10.

Chapter 1: Simple Mark Making will take you through your first few experiments with the pyrography pen. By the time you finish this chapter, you'll be ready to make a set of simple coasters. Page 24.

Chapter 2: Basic Decoration Techniques shows you how to link together the marks you've learned to make in order to decorate an object. Page 44.

Chapter 3: Silhouettes walks you through the creation of a basic decorating technique. Silhouettes will hone your shading and mark-making skills. Page 60.

Chapter 4: Drawing with Fire will show you the subtleties of drawing using a pyrography pen. You'll be able to create a beautiful landscape utilizing the skills you learn here. Page 78.

Chapter 5: Texture and Pattern exposes the world of possibilities for covering a surface with pyrography. You can make a piece of wood look like an ancient stone surface, or even use a microscopic view of coral to decorate an object. Page 98.

Chapter 6: Lettering introduces a vital component of any personalized design: the letters. You'll learn the important techniques of how to create legible letters. Page 110.

Chapter 7: Portraits illustrates the basics for creating a realistic image of a person or animal using pyrography. Page 134.

Chapter 8: Ideas and Inspiration closes the book with pages chock-full of ideas to utilize your newfound pyrography skills. If you're stumped for project inspiration, you won't be for long! Page 158.

Check out the back for useful information on woods for pyrography (Appendix A, page 199), texture ideas (Appendix B, page 201), and resources (page 204).

Getting Started

The word *pyrography* literally means "writing with fire," and it is a tradition that dates back hundreds of years. Luckily, the people who still practice the craft today are not termed pyromaniacs! There is something very raw about creating images from heat or fire: the first few strokes I made burning patterns into wood when I was at school reminded me of cavemen painting crude images onto rocks with burned twigs.

The following pages will fill you in on the options available in pyrography machines and how to choose the right one for you. Also covered are types of materials that will (and won't!) take well to being decorated with pyrography work. Safety, maintenance, finishes, and more—it's all here.

Pyrography is a rewarding craft to learn, regardless of your previous experience or artistic ability. With practice, you will be able to create beautiful gifts and items, such as this wooden plate decorated with a Celtic knot design.

Pyrography Machines

Pyrography is also often known as *woodburning* or *pokerwork*, the latter deriving from the metal pokers used during the Victorian era that were heated to use as drawing tools. The irons would have cooled very quickly and required re-heating frequently between applications, making the process of creating a piece of art very slow and meticulous. Fortunately, pyrography machines—which heat quickly and stay hot—are available to those wishing to pursue the craft of pyrography today. Modern pyrography machines have been designed to be easier to use, requiring less preparation and with improved safety in mind. Most standard pyrography machines are comprised of a transformer or power unit with a mains adaptor. The pens for these units are usually separate components that plug into the mains unit. Some units may have sockets or adapters for more than one pen to be used at once: this can be advantageous if you are working with more than one style of nib on the same design, as you do not need to let the machine cool and change the nib as often. Other manufacturers produce pens with fixed nibs so that you need to swap from pen to pen to create different marks and textures: this may seem time-consuming but it does mean that you do not have to allow for cooling down.

Some craft outlets sell basic pyrography kits for beginners, which are often supplied with a basic instruction book and some sample materials to work on. They generally take the form of large pens that have an adaptor incorporated directly into the body of the pen itself, without a separate power unit.

Modern pyrography machines are generally available in two formats: the solid point machine or the hot wire version. The benefits of modern machines are quickly apparent: most pyrography machines now have adjustable heat settings and a range of pen tips that can be used to create different effects or marks. Due to the nature of the work for which they are intended, they are usually sturdy and robust machines, made from strong plastics or steel to ensure the interior is well protected. Though both types of machine are useful, they do have their pros and cons.

Solid point machines

Solid point machines have solid metal tips, which usually come in a range of sizes and shapes to produce different marks and effects. The machines usually resemble a soldering iron in their physical appearance. They can take some time to heat up depending on the size and thickness of each individual tip. The nibs are often held in place by a screw or similar fitting, which makes them fairly simple to remove and change. Solid point kits are the most widely available type of pyrography machine and tend to be cheaper, too. As the machines generally don't have a separate base unit, the heating element is inside the pen itself, so they tend to be larger: this may be an advantage or a disadvantage depending on your personal preferences. Many people find it difficult or awkward working with a pen where their hand is quite a distance away from the working nib. Personal preference and comfort are valid factors to consider when you buy.

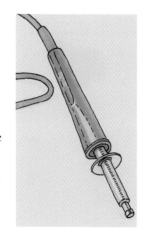

Solid point pyrography machines are similar in appearance to soldering irons, comprising of a pen with solid metal tips and an electrical flex to connect it to the mains. Some pyrography machines are supplied with a range of different tips in various shapes and sizes.

Hot wire machines

Hot wire machines have a metal wire nib, which heats up very quickly like the element in a lightbulb. Because of this, the temperature is very easy to adjust for creating different grades and qualities of mark. There are a range of different wire nibs available in the same way as the solid point tips, which are all suitable for different effects such as fine lines, textures, broad area shading, and so on. The range and selection of ready-made tips produced by North American manufacturers is extensive, so you are guaranteed you will find a suitable nib for any mark you have in mind. It is also possible to buy lengths of pyrography wire from craft outlets to create your own nibs by shaping and filing: this practice is most common with pyrography machines produced in Europe. Using shaped nibs you have made for specific purposes can be rewarding, cost-effective, and time-saving. Some hot wire machines require swapping entire pens, rather than just the nib. Most hot wire machines have a separate base unit where the heating mechanism is located, so the pen itself can be smaller, lighter, and often easier to handle as a result.

I have always preferred to use a hot wire pyrography machine. I believe they are easier to use, quicker to heat and cool down, and more adaptable for a range of situations and techniques. This is only personal preference, and most pyrography techniques are essentially the same in principle no matter which machine you use. However, please be aware that most of the designs in this book have been created using a hot wire machine.

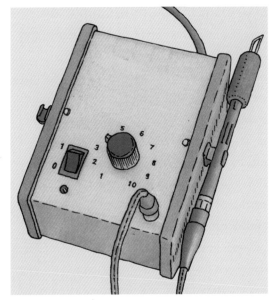

Hot wire pyrography machines consist of a base unit with an adjustable temperature dial. The pens are often separate components that are plugged into the unit. Some machines are able to power more than one pen at a time.

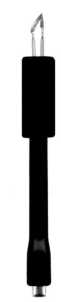

This example of a separate pyrography pen shows a fixed nib at the top. The plastic body is attached to the base unit by a separate electrical lead, allowing different pens to be used with the same machine.

Pyrography nibs are available in a wide range of shapes and sizes, each with their own particular use and abilities.

Solid point nib

Pros	Cons
• Wide range of manufactured specialist nibs and tips available • Often cheaper in price and more readily available to purchase • Nibs are easy to change and do not break easily • Good for large work	• Can be slow to heat up and slower to burn the surface • Pens are often larger, heavier, and harder to handle, with a greater distance between hand and nib • Some machines use fixed nibs, offering less variety in marks • Handle can heat up if the element is contained within • Less adjustability and control • Not well suited to detailed and fine work

Hot wire nib

Pros	Cons
• Heats up and cools down quickly • Wide range of manufactured specialist nibs available • Possible to make your own shaped nibs from Nichrome wire • Pens are generally smaller, lighter, and easier to handle • More likely to have an adjustable temperature setting • Burns the wood more easily and quickly • Pen has no heating element within so will be cooler to hold • Good for detailed work	• Machines are more expensive and less commonly available • Specialist nibs may be expensive • Nibs can break more easily • Pens can sometimes break or develop a fault with regular use, particularly around areas where the nibs are fitted to the pen

Choosing a Pyrography Machine

Selecting an appropriate pyrography machine can be difficult, as they are generally not widely available. As you may often wish to use them for prolonged periods of time, it is essential that you select a comfortable piece of equipment. It would be ideal if you were able to locate a craft supply store in your locality with a range of pyrography machines in stock, so that you could "try before you buy." Unfortunately, this is usually not the case for the majority of people, and I have always had to buy my pyrography machines online through Internet craft supply websites. The benefit of these sites is they are usually very informative and you can find out a great deal of information about a particular make or model through searching for reviews from other crafters on the Net. Prices can vary as well, depending on whether you want to buy a basic pyrography craft kit for beginners or a more advanced machine. If you do buy your pyrography machine over the Internet, make sure you have selected a model with an appropriate power supply set-up for the country you are based in.

The pyrography pen is held in basically the same way as a normal writing pen or pencil, but it is manipulated in a much slower and more controlled manner. It is, therefore, important you are comfortable holding and moving the tool for longer periods of time. Think about the type of pen you prefer to write with and see if the pyrography pen matches it in terms of basic dimension. Do you prefer using a short or long pen? Do you prefer to write with a chunky pen or one that is slimmer in diameter? Do you like a heavy pen or something light? Keeping these considerations in mind may assist you in choosing a machine that is suitable. The pen will become like a quality fountain pen with time: the grip and feel will become individual to you. Certain nibs or points may wear slightly to suit the angle you hold the pen at and the pressure you apply when you

work. Using the pyrography pen should feel as smooth and natural as writing with your favorite normal pen. If it does not feel comfortable, or if holding it is awkward, then you will not be able to work to your full potential.

Protection from heat is another factor to consider when shopping for a pyrography machine. A good quality pyrography pen handle should be well-insulated against heat. Some pens are designed with a formed ridge or separate guard to prevent the risk of your fingers coming into contact with the metal section at the end, which obviously heats up to a high temperature while you are working.

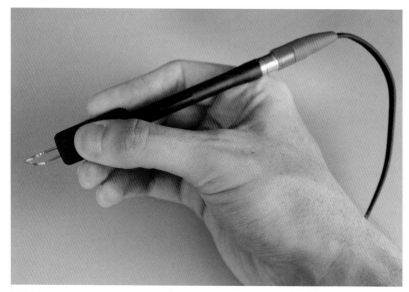

Hold the pyrography pen in exactly the same way that you hold a normal writing pen. If your fingers are too far back or you hold the pen awkwardly, you will not feel comfortable and your work will suffer as a consequence.

Photograph courtesy of Razertip.

Many pens feature some form of protection to protect against the heat of the nib. Some use a special foam guard (above) to insulate the pen, while others may have a raised guard or lip to prevent fingers from getting too close to the hot nib.

Additional Equipment

As well as your pyrography machine of choice, the following other tools or items of equipment may prove useful to you while working:

- A range of standard pencils for drawing designs onto your material. You may prefer to use automatic or mechanical pencils with refillable lead. The delicate nature of the line that these provide can be more suited to accurate work, and they are also less prone to smudge. If you choose to use a traditional pencil, you will need a good quality pencil sharpener to keep your pencils in good condition.

- A good eraser for correcting the inevitable mistakes that will occur! I tend to use a soft eraser as it is less likely to mark or damage the surface you are working on.

- A range of sandpapers to assist with correcting more serious mistakes and for the preparation of wooden surfaces.

- A ruler and set of compasses to assist in marking up designs. These are particularly useful for accuracy when working with borders or other geometric shapes.

- A set of geometric stencils can be very useful if you repeatedly use simple shapes such as circles or ovals.

- An appropriate screwdriver and set of pliers for changing the nibs or wires on your pyrography machine.

- A selection of jeweler's needle files, which can be used to create your own shaped nibs for hot wire machines.

The basic essentials in terms of drawing equipment for any new pyrographer (from left to right): a steel ruler, an eraser, a selection of pencils, a craft scalpel, a pair of compasses, an automatic (or mechanical) pencil, tracing paper, and masking tape.

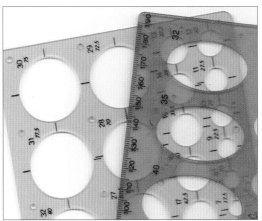

Geometric stencils can be very handy for drawing small shapes such as circles or ovals.

You will also find the following tools very useful for preparing and maintaining materials and equipment (from left to right): a selection of sandpaper (from coarse to fine), a pair of pliers, a set of jeweler's needle files, and a flat-headed screwdriver.

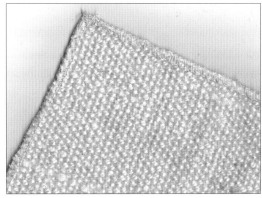

You can purchase protective mats to protect your work surface from the heat of the pyrography pen.

- A protective board to avoid damage to your table or desk. I suggest heavy duty cardboard or a solid piece of plywood. This can be a scrap piece of material that you can replace once it becomes too pitted or grubby for further use. You can also purchase a heat-resistant mat designed to cope with extremely high temperatures.
- Sheets of tracing paper for transferring designs onto your material. You can use graphite paper if you wish, but it is a little more expensive.
- A roll of masking tape for keeping the tracing paper or stencil in place when you are transferring designs onto your materials. Also use it to mask off areas you wish to keep clean or protect in some way while you are working.
- A good craft knife or scalpel for correcting errors made by burning a surface too much.
- A supply of steel wool for cleaning pyrography nibs after prolonged periods of burning. You can also use an old craft knife blade to remove dirty deposits from the pen nibs.
- A small anvil and hammer, if you really enjoy making and shaping your own nibs. They can be used to flatten wire nibs into fine flat edges or delicate points.
- A supply of soft cloths for wiping dust and grit away from your working surfaces, as well as for applying finishing treatments.
- A selection of different oils or varnishes for finishing your work.
- An electric fan to remove the smoke as you burn.
- A good electric light so you can see clearly as you work.

We will cover other materials and media that you can combine with your pyrography designs, such as paints, colored pencils, and other accessories. These are not essential as you learn the basics of pyrography, but they do provide the scope for broadening the potential of your work.

Materials for Pyrography Use

It is possible to use pyrography on a range of different materials, such as wood, leather, paper, card, cork, and gourds. My favorite woods to work on are beech and sycamore. Both are pale in color with a fine grain, which means they provide a perfect contrast with the pyrography marks. I have also worked on pine, oak, basswood/lime, maple, and several other species. Appendix A at the back of this book features a guide to many common woods and their suitability for pyrography. Below are some considerations for selecting materials for your pyrography projects.

Wood slabs

A piece of wood was once alive, perhaps part of a sturdy oak or an elegant willow tree. It is easy for people to look at a knot or similar mark as an unsightly blemish or fault, but this is mainly due to the smooth perfection of other manmade materials we are surrounded with on a day-to-day basis, such as plastics or metal. The tree existed and, therefore, has a history of its life. Each mark may be the result of a hard winter, a lightning strike during a bad storm, the loss of a branch, or an insect habitation. If you think of knots as unique design features instead of blemishes, a world of possibilities opens up. Many other common and uncommon "blemishes" of wood can be used in your designs. Splits, cracks, the swirling grain of a burl, small holes created by burrowing insects, and the dark irregular marks of spalting (showing the progress of a fungus inside the log) can all become useful and desirable design elements.

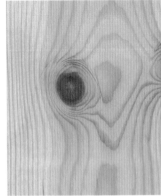

Knots are a natural feature of wood. Some people see them as an imperfection on a working surface but their appearance can be used to your advantage at times.

Spalting, caused by fungus, can create beautiful and interesting black lines in wood.

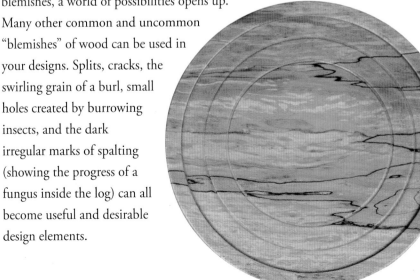

There is a massive range of wooden craft blanks available to buy for pyrography use. Visit your local arts and crafts store, or look for online retailers that will ship directly to your address.

Wooden blanks

Wooden blanks are ideal for use with pyrography and easily found at many craft suppliers and art shops. These include key ring fobs, plates, boxes, eggs, plaques, bowls, napkin rings, chopping boards, kitchen implements, place mats, picture frames, toys, and much more. Many of the step-by-step guides in this book use such blanks, so you can easily purchase the materials required to attempt the projects in this book and to generally improve your own skills.

Second-hand items

You may also wish to browse second-hand stores, junk shops, or antique retailers in order to locate items with more of a story behind them. Similarly, you may find that particular item you are looking for on an online Internet auction website. You can often pick up items in this way at very low prices, which is great if you are worried about making a mistake. Remember, one man's junk is another man's treasure… keep your eyes peeled at the next garage sale and you may find an ideal canvas for your developing talents!

The only consideration that you will need to take is if a wooden item has already been treated or finished in some way. Most varnishes or lacquers release unpleasant fumes when burned with a pyrography tool. As a general rule, the more plastic-like the finish on the wood, the more likely it is that the fumes will be horrible and possibly dangerous to your health. Prepare the area you wish to decorate by sanding it down to the bare wood before applying the pyrography design.

Plywood

Plywoods can be used for pyrography, as the surface layers are often pale in color, which is ideal for contrast. The only issue to bear in mind is the thickness of the layer you are working on, so you don't work too deep. You could possibly reveal a layer of a different color, and the glue used to sandwich the plywood may produce unpleasant fumes when heated.

Leather

Leather can be a very rewarding surface to work on. It requires a lower temperature setting than wood. Be careful which type of leather you select to use, as some tanning methods use chemicals that are harmful when released as fumes during burning. Most craft suppliers make items such as key fobs and bookmarks from vegetable-tanned leather, which is safe to burn, supple, and available in a range of pale colors for contrast.

An example of a pyrography design on a piece of vegetable-tanned leather.

Paper, card stock, and cork

It is also possible to use pyrography on paper and card stock. Every technique described in this book for use on wood will also apply. However, this process requires more caution and concentration than wood, as the material is more delicate and there is a risk of burning through the surface. It is best to have a piece of scrap paper on hand so you can practice and get the hang of the way the paper reacts to the application of the heated nib. Paper and card stock are cheap and widely available: check your local art store. Many of the same principles apply for burning on cork, as it is a very soft material that burns quite easily.

Pyrography on paper can provide a stunning contrast, but care must be taken when applying the heat due to the delicate nature of the material.

Cork can give great shading effects (such as the mottled coat of this rabbit), but is not the best surface for detailed work or fine lines. It is very soft and burns easily.

Materials to avoid

Woods with a very strong grain can be difficult to work on: the heat of the pyrography pen can travel along with the grain against the intended direction of the mark. This means that a line may not appear even or neat, despite the best intentions and efforts of the craftsperson.

Soft and sappy woods, such as pine, can be a little tricky to work with due to the sap or resin contained within. The heat of the pen can make the wood weep a little, causing the pen nib to get clogged up or sticky. This does not mean these woods are completely useless for pyrography; it just means you need to exercise more patience while working on them, and clean your pyrography pen more frequently. Woods like this are often best suited to bold, simple designs rather than intricate artwork with a lot of fine detail.

MDF (medium density fiberboard) and similar materials should be avoided above all else! These materials are made of compressed wood fragments combined with strong glues or chemicals at high pressure to make something almost plastic in its characteristics. Most of the chemicals used in the manufacture of manmade composite materials can give off harmful or toxic fumes when heated. Of course, plastics themselves are also not suitable for pyrography.

Safety Advice

Pyrography machines use electricity to become hot—so you've got the obvious concerns that go with electricity and heat. There are also a few other safety items that you might not think of until you've experienced them. Please read through the following information and make sure you stay safe while using your pyrography machine!

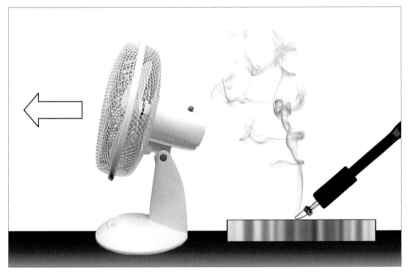

Positioning an electrical fan so that it points away from your working area will draw the smoke away from you without affecting the working temperature of your pyrography machine.

Ventilation

Work in a well-ventilated area wherever possible. Burning any material creates smoke and fumes, and working with a pyrography machine to draw usually brings the crafter directly over their material of choice. Work near a window, or consider placing an electric fan near your work area to move the smoke away from you. Rather than pointing the fan at you, place the fan near but facing away to draw the smoke away from you without the moving air cooling the hot pen nib and reducing the working temperature. If you do not have a fan, you may wish to consider wearing a mask or pair of goggles if necessary. The smoke created can make your eyes water, or possibly cause any respiratory problems from which you suffer to worsen.

Fire safety

Never use your machine near chemicals, flammable substances, or other potential fuel sources. Despite the relatively small size, the heat in a pyrography pen can still be intense enough to cause a fire if not used cautiously.

Smoke alarms

Avoid working near smoke alarms. Your neighbors will not appreciate the piercing shriek of your alarms on a regular basis when you really get into your craft sessions!

Changing nibs

Whichever machine you choose, remember to ensure the tips are completely cool before changing them by hand. The glowing red heat of a hot wire nib is a very clear indication it is too hot to handle, but this disappears within seconds of the machine being switched off. The nib will still be too hot to touch for some time, so leave the kit alone for at least 10 minutes or so before attempting any alterations. If in doubt, press the nib on a piece of scrap paper: if the paper does not burn or become discolored in any way, you may be able to handle the nib. Caution is the best advice I can give; otherwise, your hands and fingers may soon be covered with small nib-shaped scars.

It is often very hard to tell if a pyrography nib is still hot, so please be cautious. Treat all nibs as if they are hot unless you have verified they are definitely not. Test a nib on a piece of scrap wood or paper first before touching it.

Hot pens

If your pen does get hot and uncomfortable to hold during a sustained period of burning, turn the machine off and put the pen down. Allowing the pen to cool for a few minutes is recommended. If your machine uses interchangeable pens, you can always consider swapping pens at this point to keep going. Otherwise, take the opportunity to have a refreshment break and rest your eyes while the pen cools down, rather than soldiering on in discomfort.

If a pen handle feels very hot during use, turn it off, let it cool, and check for damage. The plastic casing may have become cracked or broken. Damaged pens can be a hazard and should be replaced immediately.

Protect your fingers

Make sure you are always careful when burning into small items that you need to hold in your hand, such as key ring fobs or small trinket boxes. Working on large flat pieces of wood can be very straightforward, as it is easy to rest the heel of your palm on the surface to support you as you work. It is easy to become absorbed in your work and forget how close you are to your fingertips with smaller items. Work patiently and adjust your grip as you work to ensure your fingers are always as far as possible from the tip of the pen while you burn.

Take care when burning small items. Make sure your fingers are always as far as possible from the area where you are working with the hot nib.

Twisted wires

Ensure that the electrical flex linking the pen to the pyrography machine itself does not become too twisted when you constantly adjust the way that you hold the pen. This may inhibit or restrict your movement at a vital point in the burning process, which could result in an error or (even worse) you burning your fingers! If it is getting a little twisted, turn the machine off and allow the pen to cool, then unplug the pen and straighten the flex. You will then be able to plug it back into the base unit and start again unhindered.

Temporary pen storage

Always know where your pyrography pen is and make sure it is used safely. Most pyrography machines have a clip or stand attached so the pen can be placed securely inside when not in use to reduce the risk of injury or accidents. If you do not have such a feature, you may be able to use a container or stand of some sort that is made from a material that does not conduct heat.

Otherwise, it is better to be safe than sorry and turn the pen off when not in use, even for a short period of time. This is definitely the best guideline if you have children in the house, as they may try to touch the equipment while it is still hot.

Make sure the hot nib is never left or held in a way that might bring it into contact with the electrical cable linking the machine to the mains power. This may result in damage to your pyrography machine or harm to yourself or your home.

Photograph courtesy of Razertip.

Many pyrography machines are fitted with a hook or clip to hold the pen when not in use, so you do not inadvertently burn your work surface or yourself!

Other problems

If you have any problems with your pyrography machine, check the instruction manual for your particular make and model. These guides often include a troubleshooting guide for common faults that can be resolved easily. If the fault appears serious, make sure you get it examined or repaired by a qualified engineer. This is particularly important if the fault appears to be of an electrical nature: if the machine displays any sparks or makes any buzzing noises, turn it off and disconnect it immediately before seeking professional advice. I would suggest you contact the manufacturer to see if they have any servicing agreements, or make enquiries with the retailer that you purchased it from.

My first pyrography machine developed a fault while I was in the middle of an important project. There appeared to be a problem with the connection inside the power unit, which was remedied by placing a pressure or weight on it. In my rush to finish the project without waiting for my new machine to arrive, I used an easily available pressure source to make the machine work. Unfortunately, the chosen pressure source was my knee, which I found was not exactly heat resistant, and I still have a small scar there to this day resulting from the burn. Please take note of my mistake and learn from it!

Nib Maintenance

As you work through a pyrography design, the nib of the pen will be used to burn the surface in a variety of ways. Over time, carbon deposits and ash will build up on the nib. This can reduce the working temperature of the nib so that you find it harder to burn in a certain way, or you find it takes a longer time to create a certain effect. The deposits can clog up the nib, causing it to snag or dig in as you work across the surface. Any of these issues can ruin the quality of the line or mark you are trying to achieve. Cleaning the nib regularly will prevent these problems from having a detrimental effect on your design work.

Quick cleaning methods

Tapping the nib on a metal surface can dislodge most deposits if you want to give the nib just a quick clean while you are working. I have an old flat-headed screwdriver that is sufficient: the lightly pitted surface means I can also run the nib across it to remove the unwanted grit.

Special tip cleaners enable you to clean the nibs whether they are hot or cold. These are usually in the form of a blade fixed into a solid base with a protective cover. The nib is drawn through a pair of fixed blades or one blade with a V-shaped notch cut in it. Because the blade is fixed into a protective base that does not conduct heat, this type of device can avoid wasting time unnecessarily by waiting for tips to cool before you can clean them. You can literally swipe the tip through the blades and go back to your burning. This is the best way to clean your nibs, in my opinion, as it does not affect the nib in the same way that frequent abrasion does.

Cool-down cleaning methods

Prior to cleaning any nib thoroughly, turn the machine off and allow it to cool down so it is not hot to touch. Coarse steel wool is an ideal tool for cleaning nibs: just give the nib a quick brush through the wool several times to remove the ash and dust. You can also use an old craft knife blade or very fine sandpaper to lightly scrape any stubborn deposits off the nib.

Reshaping

You may find your favorite nibs become worn, pitted, or dulled with time and constant use. An oilstone can be used to gently add the sharp edge back onto a bladed nib. You may not be able to sharpen the edge of hot wire nibs on more than a few occasions, as they are delicate and will weaken after several treatments. Solid point nibs are much more robust in this respect and will last much longer with even the most vigorous cleaning and reshaping.

Finishing Your Work

How to protect your finished work depends on the nature of the object you have created. If you are not sure what effects a particular varnish or oil may have on the wood surface or tones of your pyrography design, I would always recommend trying a small area on a piece of scrap wood first. It is much better to spend a bit of time doing this, rather than inadvertently ruining a finished piece of work at the final stages. This is particularly important in the future if you start to combine other materials, such as paint or ink, with your pyrography. There would be no bigger frustration than completing a design only to see the colors run when you start varnishing.

Keep in mind while applying that most varnishes have guidelines that show how long before a coat is touch dry, and how long it takes to dry completely. If you do not follow the instructions, the lower coats may not dry fully which affects each subsequent coat: sometimes the finished effect can appear rippled or dull. You cannot rush the process, so make sure you allow

Use a large soft paintbrush to apply varnishes to your crafted items, and remember to allow time to dry between coats. Always follow the directions on the container of the particular brand that you are using.

Apply Danish oil or other finishes to wooden items with a soft cloth.

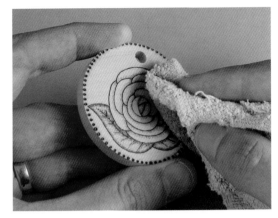

Danish oil gives the wood a pleasing warm luster. The right side of this fob has been treated, while the left side is plain wood.

Clear varnish

As Danish oil or similar substances change the color of the wood slightly, you may find you lose some of the contrast a pale wood provides. If you wish to keep the contrast in your design, it is possible to use a clear varnish to protect the wood without affecting the shade or tone. Most craft suppliers or art shops sell clear water-based varnishes that are ideal for protecting the wood, and are usually available in either satin, matte, or gloss finishes to suit your individual preference. These varnishes also protect the wood from the natural oils of our hands, so consider using these if you are creating an item that will be well-handled.

Outdoor pieces

Pyrography items for outdoor use have their own issues that need to be considered when finishing the piece. The marks burned into the wood can fade with time when exposed to strong sunlight or other elements of the weather. I use a hard-wearing yacht varnish, also known as spar or marine varnish, to finish my outdoor creations. It creates a tough seal around the wood that protects it from damage by water. It is advisable to apply at least 3-4 coats of these varnishes to ensure the best protection possible.

It is possible to purchase yacht varnish with ultra-violet light inhibitors, reducing the effects of strong sunlight. If you create such an outdoor piece, I would suggest applying another coat of yacht varnish every 2-3 years to keep up the protection level and to repair any damage to the previous coats. It is always the best practice to consider where the item is placed: perhaps a particular wall is shaded well at most points of the day, or there may be an alcove or porch that offers good protection from the sun and rain.

enough time to let each coat dry fully before you start the next application. Use a broad soft brush and apply the varnish sparingly. It is better to build up the layers gradually rather than applying too much at once, as this can result in drips or puddles, which do not dry particularly well and ruin the finished appearance.

Danish oil

Most of the items I create are for household use or display, and I have found that treating them with several coats of Danish oil is the best way of finishing them. It gives the wood a warm glowing luster that enhances the rich tones of the pyrography marks. Danish oil can simply be applied using a soft cloth or tissue. Once you have rubbed the oil into the wood, simply allow it to dry naturally in a well-ventilated area.

Chapter 1

Simple Mark Making

After reading the Getting Started section, you should now have figured out what type of pyrography machine you want and have it in hand. This chapter will help you sort out making marks. Wood grain, holding your pen, different types of marks—everything you need to create your first successful pyrography marks is explained here.

These turned wooden eggcups were decorated with very simple patterns using the most basic lines and marks.

Hot Wire Nibs

The simplest way to make a pyrography mark is to press down a hot wire nib and then lift it back up—effectively creating a pyrography stamper. Imagine using a ball-point nib to press onto a piece of wood to create a small woodburned circle—that's the essence of this technique. However, there are many pyrography tips available that make it easy to create all sorts of other marks. A quick scan over this page will show you some examples of the types of marks that can be made using only a few nibs. You can select nibs from the enormous catalog available from retailers, or you can create your own.

The four essential nibs

It is not essential for a beginner to purchase every nib possible to get a satisfactory range of marks, and I would say experimentation with a few basic nibs produces a vast range of marks that are ultimately more rewarding. For the first year of my pyrography crafting, I used nothing more than basic pyrography wire shaped to suit my own requirements for each specific design. My top four essential nibs for beginners are a general writing nib, a spoon point nib, a broader shading nib, and a blade point or skew. With these four nibs alone, you are able to create a range of marks and lines. After experimenting with these four nibs, as I have done, you will also be able to learn what marks you particularly like and will use most frequently—you will then know how best to spend your money if you buy a specialist nib.

Writing nibs have a simple bent tip. Their usefulness lies in their versatility and the way they can be moved across the working surface. Writing nibs work well for drawing and making dots, spirals, lines, text, and other irregular lines and marks.

An example of some of the marks that can be made when you experiment with a writing nib.

An example of some of the marks that can be made when you experiment with a spoon point nib.

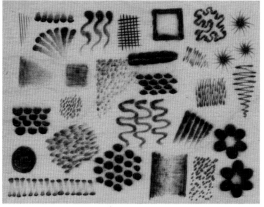
An example of some of the marks that can be made when you experiment with a shading nib.

The writing nib has a rounded end that allows it to move more fluidly over the surface in any number of directions, without digging in as a blade does.

Photograph courtesy of Razertip.

A spoon point is a versatile shading nib. The bowl allows for soft shading marks to be made while the edge can be used to make crisp lines.

Photograph courtesy of Razertip.

A spear shader can be used to shade in tight corners where other shading nibs might be too broad.

Photograph courtesy of Razertip.

Photograph courtesy of Razertip.

The skew is a typical bladed nib, ideally suited for crisp lines and fine marks.

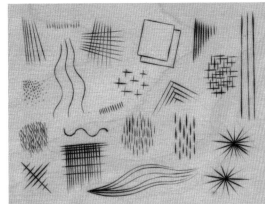

An example of some of the marks that can be made when you experiment with a bladed nib.

Spoon points are very versatile nibs able to create both lines and shading effects over smaller areas. They are bowl-shaped as the name suggests. The soft underside of the bowl can be used for delicate shading and filling in areas of tone. The thin edge of the spoon can be used to make linear marks, and therefore is useful for cross-hatching and other similar effects. If used patiently and sensitively, it can be used to mark out sharp edges and to make softer areas with no edges at all.

Shading nibs are often broader in profile to cover as much surface area as possible with a minimum of effort. They may be shaped to resemble a spear, chisel, circle, or spade, or they may be formed using a coil of thinner metal to create a larger working point. They work very well for covering larger areas with tone and texture.

Blade points have a more defined straight edge and are used to create sharp lines and associated textures. They are good for creating detailed work, such as outlines, fine texture, particularly detailed designs, or lettering.

Nib shapes

Photograph courtesy of Razertip.

Feather former nibs are constructed with fine ridges or grooves that can be used to create the delicate textures for birds and similar surface textures. They are available in a range of sizes, shapes, and grades of line density.

A range of shaped nibs is available to purchase for use with hot wire pyrography machines. Each nib has its own individual mark, purpose, and associated techniques. You may find a certain nib gives you exactly the texture or mark you are looking for, and you will build up your own personal tool kit of nibs with time as you develop your own style. It is possible to purchase nibs that create a specific texture or give the effect of a certain surface, such as bird feathers. Obviously, some points are made specifically for certain pyrography machines so make sure you do your research on the Internet or with a crafts supplier before you make any purchases. It's a good idea to check what is available on a regular basis as there are often new developments or products available in the pyrography market.

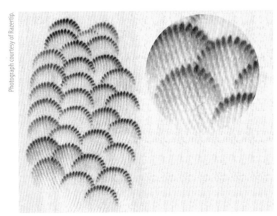

Photograph courtesy of Razertip.

Feather former nibs can be used in a structured manner, moving across a surface to create a layered pattern.

Examples of Nibs Available for Purchase

Large skew. Fine detail and long straight lines.

Medium skew. Fine detail and crisp, sharp lines.

Small skew. Fine detail and sharp lines on a small scale.

Extra small skew. Fine and extreme detail.

Small long skew. Fine detail where other skews may struggle to reach.

Tight round. General use on flat surfaces.

Large round. Lines on uneven or concave surfaces.

Medium round. Lines and detail on flat or slightly curved surfaces.

Small round. Fine detail on small flat or curved surfaces, as well as texturing.

Extra small round. Fine detailed work.

Round shader. Shading and blocking in areas of different sizes. Available in a range of sizes.

Large flat skew. General work. Allows you to hold your hand closer to the tip as compared to a regular skew.

Medium flat skew. General detail work. Allows you to hold your hand closer to the tip as compared to a regular skew.

Small flat skew. Fine detail work. Allows you to hold your hand closer to the tip as compared to a regular skew.

Spear. General work, detailing, texturing, and shading. Available in a range of sizes.

Wide groove medium spear. More robust work compared to the regular spear.

Medium spear shader. Patterning and surface effects. Good for shading and texture.

Medium/Small spear shader. Patterning and surface effects. Good for finer shading and texture.

Small spear shader. Patterning and surface effects. Good for detailed shading and texture.

Small long spear shader. Shading in areas that may be difficult to reach with a regular spear shader.

Photographs courtesy of Razertip.

Photographs courtesy of Razertip

Large wide chisel. General use, straight lines, stamping, and shading effects.

Large chisel. General use, straight lines, stamping, and shading effects.

Medium chisel. General use, straight lines, detail, stamping, and shading effects.

Small chisel. General use, fine detail, stamping, and shading effects.

Extra small chisel. Extremely fine detail and marks.

Calligraphy chisel. Broad and fine strokes needed to create calligraphic lettering. Available in a range of different widths.

Brass calligraphy nib. Slightly rounded to allow a smoother movement across the surface as you write. Available in a range of different widths.

Chisel shader. General shading techniques. Available in a range of sizes.

Large round skew. Detailed and textural work across a range of surfaces.

Medium round skew. Detailed and textural work across a range of surfaces, including small areas.

Small round skew. Fine detail and textures including confined spaces and smaller areas.

Extra small round skew. Extremely fine detail and textural work on the smallest of areas.

Burnisher. General use and burnishing surfaces. Good for soft detail and shading effects.

Writing tip. For writing and marks that change direction fluidly across a surface. Available in a range of sizes.

General nib. Suitable for writing, shading, texturing, small marks, and burnishing. Available in a range of sizes.

Dual line. Creating fine parallel lines and texturing. Available in a range of sizes.

Curved spear. Allows you to reach into awkward areas due to the angle and shape. Available in a range of sizes.

Sharp angle medium skew. Extremely fine detailing and lines.

Knife. General versatile use on a range of surfaces. Available in a range of sizes.

Large skew shader. Shading and line work. Available in both left- and right-handed versions.

Large skew shader. This version has a bend in the shaft to allow a different working angle when shading or making lines. Available in both left- and right-handed versions.

Small skew shader. Texturing and shading. Available in both left- and right-handed versions.

45° shader. Shading techniques where a 45° angle is required. Available in a range of sizes.

Coarse detail. Wider marks, coarse lines, and shading effects. Available in a range of sizes.

Multi use. Versatile nib for texture, patterns, shading, carving, writing, and detail. Available in a range of sizes.

Medium spoon shader. Great all-around nib, which can be used on its edge for fine lines or on the bowl for shading.

Small spoon shader. Finer lines and shading smaller, detailed areas.

V-brand. Making patterns and consistent V shapes. Available in a range of sizes.

Transfer shader. General shading and heat transfer techniques, where designs are transferred onto the working surface. Available in a range of sizes.

Circle stamper. Textural use and patterns, through making consistent circle shapes. Available in a range of sizes.

Square stamper. Textural use and patterns, through making consistent square shapes. Available in a range of sizes.

Ball stylus. Writing, burnishing, shading, and any technique where smooth movement across the surface is required. Available in a range of sizes.

Rotating ball stylus. Writing, shading, burnishing, and the like. Similar to the tip of a ball-point pen. Available in a range of sizes.

Half scale. Used in rows to give the impression of scales and similar textures. Available in a range of sizes and shapes.

Sharp smile. Used in rows to give the impression of scales and similar sharp patterns. Available in a range of sizes and shapes.

Blunt smile. Used in rows to give the impression of scales or similar with a softer appearance. Available in a range of sizes and shapes.

Pyrography wire can be purchased in coils, straight sections, or pre-cut lengths ready to be shaped.

Photograph courtesy of Razertip.

A pyrography pen designed to hold nibs made from pyrography wire is a very versatile addition to your equipment. The nibs are held into the holding posts by small screws or bolts, and replacing them takes only a few seconds with the use of a flat-headed screwdriver.

Homemade nibs

Basic pyrography wire can be purchased in coiled lengths and cut into small sections for use as nibs. You generally need only 1⅛ to 2" (30 to 50mm) of wire for a general purpose looped nib or point, but it is dependent on the shape you wish to create. Pyrography wire is made of Nichrome (a nickel and chromium alloy) and is available in a range of thicknesses: the thinner the wire, the more detailed or defined the mark on the wood will be. Thicker wire sections are ideal for making nibs for broader areas of shading or tone. The other point to consider is broader wire will not heat up as fast as wire with a thinner section, so using broader wire can be a good technique for ensuring you do not burn the wood too heavily (something you may find happens on your first attempts!). I would definitely recommend buying a pen to hold homemade nibs for your particular pyrography machine if one is available, as it offers a lot of flexibility for the creative crafter.

It is possible to create a massive range of marks and effects using a single basic nib such as the one created in the sidebar on page 32. Because this nib has a slightly rounded end (making it easy to change direction) and a small surface area in contact with the wood, it is very versatile for writing, drawing, and shading. You can make slight alterations to the nib with ease by adjusting, bending, or shaping it. Each change will affect the amount of nib in contact with the burn surface.

- Bending the end of the nib to bring a larger section in contact with the surface you are working on will enable you to make broader marks, ideal for covering a larger area of shading.
- Filing the end of a nib to make it narrower and more pointed reduces the amount of hot metal in direct contact with the wood, which enables you to create finer lines or marks required for detailed work.

- You can also make nibs with a section of wire in contact with the wood, rather than a single point: this makes them perfect for shading larger areas or for lettering such as calligraphy.
- You may also want to bend the nib nearer to the shaft of the pen in order to increase or decrease the distance between the nib and surface of the wood: this can make the pen feel more comfortable to work with and can make the nib a little more stable in your hand.
- If you want to make a curve, fold the wire around a pen or pencil.
- The longer the length of wire, the less effectively it will heat up, and the more flimsy it will be to use.
- If the wire that you are using is slightly wavy or kinked, the contact with the wooden surface will not be even, so the patterned mark will be irregular. This may create a dotted or faded effect you can use. If you want to straighten the wire, gently squeeze it with a pair of flat-nosed pliers several times. If you change the angle you squeeze from each time, gradually working your way around the wire, you should eventually straighten it sufficiently to ensure good contact with the wood. If you have access to a small anvil or metal surface, you can always gently flatten the wire nib with a small hammer, tapping it lightly to smooth out any kinks.

You can also shape and customize any nibs that you have with needle files to make a more detailed point or defined shape. Just remember to not shape them too much, as the metal wire is fairly thin. Too much alteration may result in the wire becoming weak with heat and snapping after a relatively short period of time. This can be immensely frustrating if you then have to spend time creating a second identical nib in order to complete a project you were only halfway through!

BASIC LOOPED NIB

If you want to make your own wire nibs for a hot wire pyrography machine, follow these steps.

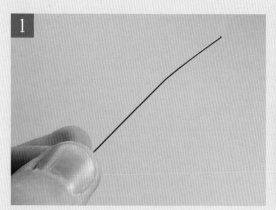

1
Cut a small section of pyrography wire, approximately 1⅛ to 2" (30 to 50mm) long.

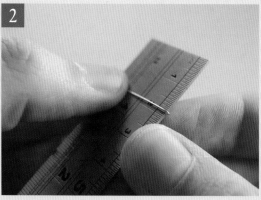

2
Fold it in half around the edge of a metal ruler. Use a pair of pliers to pinch the fold to a point.

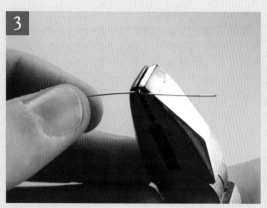

3
Bend the ends back against the side of the pliers to help form the shoulders of the nib.

4
Shape the two ends so they are parallel and at the correct distance to fit into the metal nib holders on the pyrography pen.

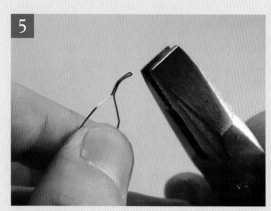

5
Shape the end of the nib to suit your requirements. This can help to increase the working area of the nib by altering the amount of metal that will be in contact with the wood.

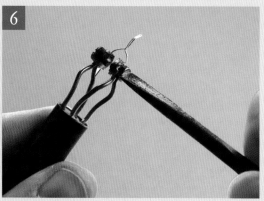

6
Fit the handmade nib into the pyrography pen and tighten the holding screws with a flat-headed screwdriver. You are ready to start burning.

Holding and Moving the Pyrography Pen

As discussed in the Getting Started section, a pyrography pen should feel natural in your hands. You should aim to hold it as you would a normal pen: if your grip is awkward or not relaxed, the unwanted tension will be reflected in the quality of the marks you make.

Proper hand position

Consider the way you hold the pen in your hand. It should be no different to the way you would usually hold a writing pen to ensure you use it in a way in which you feel most comfortable. Once the pen is in your hand, you should be able to rest the edge of your palm lightly on the surface to be burned (or the table if it is a smaller item). The pen nib should meet the surface in a natural diagonal position: if you are holding the pen almost perpendicular to the surface with your hand away from the surface, you may not be able to control the marks you make very well. This would probably result in uneven lines and areas that are heavily burned by pressing too hard with a jabbing motion, rather than a smooth flowing movement.

Rest the heel of your palm on the wood or your work surface as you burn to ensure that your pen is steady and reduce the chance of making mistakes.

Curved motions

Our hands naturally move around the pivot point our wrists provide. If you are making curved lines or marks, it is easier to work with the natural movement of your wrist than against it. To assist with this, the easiest thing to do is to turn the wooden surface as needed to ensure your hand's movements flows with the curve instead of away from it. You do not need to

Your wrist is a natural pivot and can be used to make curves that follow this movement.

work with the piece of wood in one position "the right way up" in front of you from start to finish. I often turn my work upside down, on its edge and back again hundreds of times during a session. The main thing to consider is that you can adjust whatever you need to in order to get the best mark and the best conditions to work in.

Nib choice

The choice of nib will have an impact on the way you hold the pen in your hand. For example, if you are using a spoon point to softly shade an area, you may want to check that the bowl of the nib is touching the surface and you are holding the pen to enable this without twisting your hand. Turning the pen through 180° so the bowl is facing outward and upward will mean you can then use the same nib to create more defined lines as the edge of the bowl will now be in contact with the wooden surface. Depending on the nib you are using, you will need to adjust the way you hold the pyrography pen to get the best results. But always make sure you are comfortable!

Using the point of a shading tip is useful for drawing lines. Using the broader face brings more metal into contact with the wood and creates a shading effect.

Marking the Wood

It is a good idea for anyone starting the art of pyrography to consider his or her first attempts as practice. I suggest finding some scrap pieces of wood to make your first marks on while you build up your confidence and try out your new machine. I would recommend you choose a good plain wood, such as birch or sycamore, for your first attempts, rather than a piece with knots or a strong grain pattern. You will need as blank a canvas as possible so nothing gets in your way while you attempt to master the basic techniques. Making marks may feel slightly awkward or different to start with, but you will feel more comfortable with time and experience.

This may be one of the first times you have turned on your pyrography equipment, so make sure you are fully aware of the way it operates and any safety instructions specific to the model you are using. As soon as the power has been switched on, treat the pen very carefully, as it is not often possible to see that the metal is hot. If the machine has a temperature control dial, start with the minimum setting and gradually turn the dial until you can see a slight glow on the nib. If your machine does not have a nib, check the instruction manual for details of how long the nib should take to warm up.

Factors that affect marks

Once you feel you have practiced enough to achieve a satisfactory line quality you are able to create regularly, you can start to consider the other variables that can change the appearance of pyrography marks. See sidebars on page 37 and 47.

Temperature is an obvious factor that can be adjusted readily if you have a machine with a thermostat dial. Experiment with drawing lines at different temperatures so you can see what qualities each has in their physical appearance. Too high a temperature will leave orange scorch flares around the edge of the mark. While you

may be able to use these deliberately to your benefit in some situations, they do detract from the quality of the line in detailed work or lettering. One method I often use to cool a nib for a short period of time is to blow gently on it: this saves time waiting for a nib to cool down and allows you to work with a wider variety of potential marks more quickly than relying on the machine's settings. It can also be very useful if your pyrography machine does not have an adjustable setting mechanism.

Pressure is another element with which you may experiment. While pressure can result in unsightly scorches or deep burns in the wood, you may also identify a texture or mark with a certain quality that is perfect for a design you work on sometime in the future.

Adjusting the angle of the pen or the nib will alter the amount or shape of hot metal in contact with the wood, and change the appearance of the mark. When a bladed nib is used on a surface, the length of the blade will give a straighter and crisper line than using the tip alone, due to the amount of metal in contact with the wood. The blade of such nibs can be used to cut through the figure of the wood where other nibs might catch or snag, ruining the quality of the line.

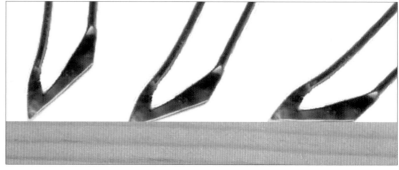

Using the length of a blade is good for long straight lines as the blade will cut through the wood and follow its own track. Using just the tip will allow you to change direction more easily and make curves or shaped marks.

PRACTICE EXERCISE: DRAW A LINE

There are a few techniques you can practice in order to learn the basic foundations of working in pyrography. The obvious place to start is with drawing a line.

It would be very difficult to draw a long continuous line across a wooden surface using a pyrography pen. The quality of the surface changes according to the figure, grain, and inherent characteristics of each type of wood. The best way to make a line is in stages. You need to re-position your hand frequently to create a longer line in small sections. Try to work with the natural movement and flow of your wrist, as this is the most comfortable way to write or draw. If you try to pull the pen in a line using the movement of your fingers toward your hand, the range of movement is a lot more limited.

The aim is to get a line that is even in tone, depth, and thickness from one end to the other. Start the line softly and slowly. Gradually introduce the nib to the wood at an angle, rather than pressing it straight down. Many pyrographers relate this process to a plane landing on a runway. Try to move at a steady and even pace across the wood: if you jerk or stop for even a split second, the heat application will be uneven and you will get blobs. When you are ready to remove the nib from the surface, do so like you started the line: lift the nib gradually as you keep moving.

Your first attempt may look uneven or ugly, but that's the whole point of practicing! The tendency for new pyrographers is to press the nib down vertically and then move sideways, which creates a heavy blobbed effect. Pressing down can gouge the wood heavily, which is hard or impossible to amend. Try to create your lines without altering the surface of the wood, as you would when drawing with a pen or pencil on thin paper. If your lines don't look smooth and even, take a look at the troubleshooting information on page 37.

Keep making more lines, working down the piece of wood as you go. As you practice, you will see the quality of the line improves as you learn what the nib will do in certain circumstances. You will find you become more confident in controlling the line quality with time and experience until it becomes second nature. You can then try other activities to improve your confidence, such as creating longer lines by joining several shorter sections together.

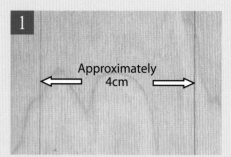

Draw two parallel tramlines or train tracks on a piece of wood to practice making lines with your pyrography pen. Do not place them too far apart for your initial attempts. Turn the pyrography machine on and set it to a medium temperature if you are using an adjustable base unit.

Approximately 4cm

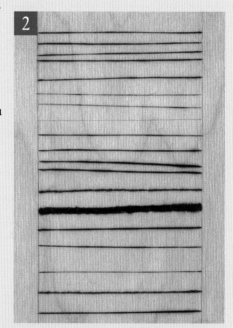

Try to create lines as smooth as possible, using a range of nibs. You will find some nibs are more suited to creating straight lines than others.

Remember to bring the pyrography pen into contact with the surface gradually to avoid making a blob or heavy burn at the start of a line. Remember to lift the pen off in the same way.

The speed that you move the pen across the wood is also a factor to consider and experiment with. A slower speed means the nib spends more time in contact with the wood making a mark. Moving the nib across the wood at high speed can be used to make light or delicate marks.

Wood features have a vast effect on pyrography, because no two pieces of wood will ever be completely the same. The natural pattern of the figure, grain, and knots can be regarded as flaws, but it is possible to be sensitive to the individual nature of the wood when creating your designs. Whether you consider these features to be flaws or assets, it is a fact that the hardness of the wood, the strength of the grain, knots, and other conditions present in the wood itself have a direct effect on the pyrography. The hard grain itself has a different heat tolerance to the softer wood surrounding it. This means the grain is usually more resistant to the heat applied, and making an even mark can be difficult as a result. It can make your lines appear dotted or uneven. The best way to address this is to practice on a scrap piece wherever possible so you can experiment with the best way to get the required result before moving to your finished piece.

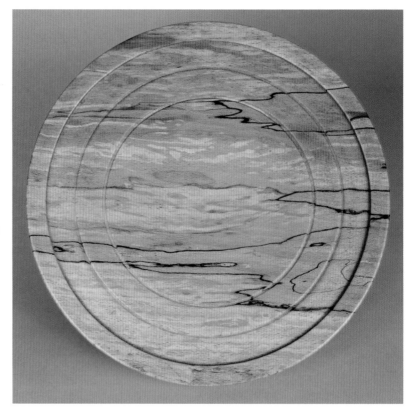

If you are having trouble getting consistent marks due to the grain or figure of the wood, take your time to build up the quality of the line or pattern. Soft grain will burn more readily than hard grain, so you will need to adjust your speed or the nib temperature to compensate for this. Use a lower temperature or a quicker speed across soft areas and the opposite for areas that are harder. If you need to go over an area several times to get the required quality of mark, then it is well worth the extra time and effort to do so rather than burning it too harshly just to save time.

This plate shows the appearance of spalting, which is a natural form of discoloration in the wood caused by fungi. Spalted areas are usually softer than the surrounding wood.

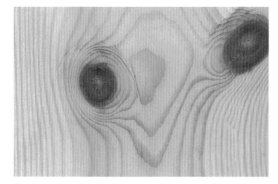

Knots are harder than surrounding areas of wood.

TROUBLESHOOTING

These images show some of the more common problems that may arise as you make your initial lines and marks.

A & G: Blobs at the start and end of a line are caused by pressing too hard, bringing the pen into contact with the wood too suddenly, or moving the pen across the surface too quickly.

B, C & J: Scorch marks during a line can be caused by inconsistent speed or moving through areas of wood grain/figure with different heat resistance qualities.

D & K: Pressing too hard as you move a writing nib across the wood can cause it to snag, catch, or jump as you draw.

E: Shading nibs can create scorch marks and uneven lines if not moved at a constant speed and pressure.

F: Thin scratchy lines are caused by low temperature setting and/or light pressure.

H: A longer line in sections that do not match up or flow well can be caused by rushing as you work.

I: Sometimes, the issue is as simple as trying to create a straight line with an inappropriate nib.

L: Using a temperature setting that is too high can cause dark scorched lines.

M: Uneven shading can be caused by rushing your work, moving the nib at inconsistent speeds, spending too long in certain areas, or differences in the surface qualities of the wood due to the figure/grain.

N: Pressing too hard while shading can create harsh depressions or burns.

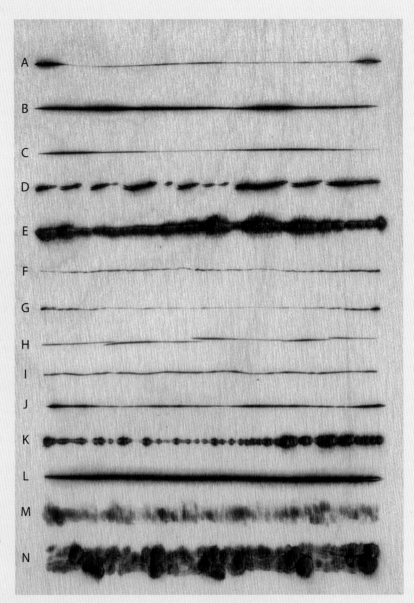

PRACTICE EXERCISES: OTHER SIMPLE MARKS

Once you feel confident with creating free lines, you can start to experiment with the other types of mark that can be produced by the pyrography nib you've been working with. Work your way through the following types of mark, practicing them until you feel confident and then experimenting with temperature, pressure, angle, and speed. You may even want to start experimenting with your own handwriting to practice your consistency, control, and technique.

ZIG-ZAGS

Bladed nibs need to be pulled back toward your hand to give the best quality of line. Trying to move a bladed nib sideways can cause it to catch or snap.

Move the wood around so that you are still drawing the blade toward you for each new section of line.

Make sure each new line matches up neatly with the previous one to make a neat corner or bend.

CURVES

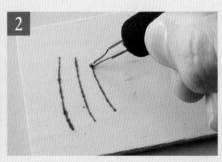

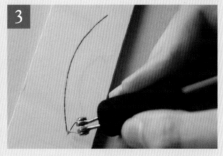

Writing nibs can be used to create lines with the natural movement of the wrist's pivot point.

Longer lines often need to be made using smaller sections to allow the hand to move into a more natural position each time before restarting.

Long sweeping curves can be difficult to draw in one attempt, so take your time and move your hand as often as necessary to get the best result.

WAVY LINES

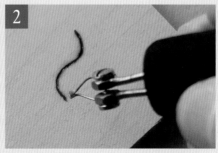

Creating wavy lines, arcs, or spirals is best done in small sections.

Move the wood around to allow for each new direction you need to draw in.

Adjust the wood as many times as you need to between each section. Make sure each new section of line matches up with the last as smoothly as possible.

DOTS

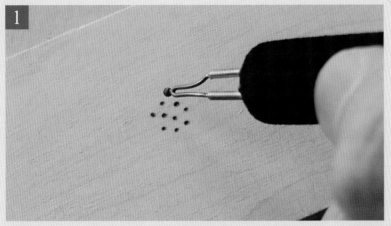

Dots can be created using a gentle dabbing motion with any shape of nib.

MARKS WITHOUT CONTACT

Set the pyrography machine to a high temperature and hold the nib a few millimeters clear of the wooden surface. You will need a steady hand for this.

The resulting mark is soft and subtle, with no indentation or impression at all in the surface of the wood.

What Next?

Patience is a key factor in pyrography, and the best work can be very time-consuming. You cannot rush your work, as the results will just not be the same. Heat is being used to change the surface of the wood, and it is hard to change something once it is burned too heavily. Therefore, it is often necessary to err on the side of caution and burn lightly at first. It is easier to make something gradually darker with a few applications than to go in too hard and waste time trying to correct it. With time, you will learn what your machine can do and how to use it, so the whole process will become more natural to you.

All of these experiments can form valuable research into what can be achieved with your new pyrography machine. Many pyrographers keep these trials for future reference, as you may one day be trying to recreate a certain style of mark for a drawing you inadvertently discovered during your initial experiments. One way to do this is to carry out experiments on pieces of wood with space to make notes by each mark, so you can easily remember how to reproduce any of the effects at a later date.

The best way to get to grips with this new craft is to experiment! Let your imagination run wild and feel free to be as playful with the techniques as you like. We will look at building marks up over an area to form controlled shading or tone during Chapter 2.

Once you have spent some time experimenting with the marks you can create with your pyrography machine, it is inevitable that you will want to start using your newfound skills to decorate and make useful items. Coasters are a perfect item for beginners: they are readily available as blanks from craft suppliers in a variety of shapes, are relatively cheap, and the small, flat surface is perfect for building up your confidence in a contained area.

Most coaster blanks are also made of woods such as birch, beech, or sycamore: the smooth, pale surface makes them ideal when starting out. The most common shape for coaster blanks are squares and circles, but you can use any shape available. Each shape will bring its own qualities and challenges when preparing a design.

Working on several identical designs to form a set is a good way of building up your confidence with the pyrography pen.

1. Preparation

The aim of this project is to practice controlling the pyrography pen and the marks you can make with it. In contrast to your practice experiments, the marks you make now will have a focus and a purpose—forming part of a decorative design. Each mark will relate not just to each other, but also to the shape and surface of the wooden coaster. The quality of each mark will need to be consistent, making this a very useful project to hone your skills.

Take time to study the trials you have made so far on your practice pieces of wood. Consider which lines and marks were your favorite to create, and which were particularly successful and appealing to the eye. It is useful to bear in mind the marks you intend to use when planning the design on the coaster.

I selected some blank round coasters for this project, but you could use any shape that you wish.

2. Design and Lay Out

The next step is to start drawing your basic design lightly onto the coaster with a sharp pencil. Use a combination of lines to make a border, such as a number of parallel lines with smaller marks between them. You can make basic parallel lines by using your finger as a running guide along the edge of the wooden item. Hold the pencil firmly in one hand and

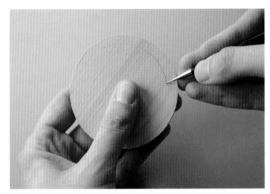

Use your fingers as a running guide to draw a pencil line parallel to the edge of the blank.

Use a ruler to add straight lines to your composition.

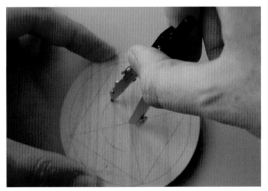

Use a pair of compasses to add circles and curved lines to the design on the blank.

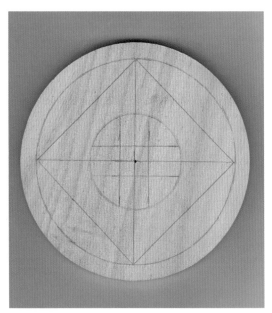

The finished design I constructed contains curves and straight lines. You can also use other types of lines, such as wavy or jagged, if you wish.

place the tip of one finger against the edge. Keep your hand rigid and run it along the edge of the coaster. Repeat this on every side of a coaster and you will have drawn a basic border. Use your ruler to help draw straight lines if you prefer: measuring the distance for each line from the edge of the wooden shape will help to keep the pattern regular and even. Use the compasses or geometric stencils if you wish to include any circles or sweeping curves in your design. You can always try drawing curves freehand if you feel confident doing so.

Try to use no more than five different sets of lines to create a simple design. Use a variety of lines that will help to build up your control with the pyrography pen. Combine straight with curved lines, wavy with jagged, flowing with broken, so that you build up a design based on contrast of form. You do not have to copy my example exactly: it is only meant to provide one example and does not include every possible type of line by all means.

3. Burn the Pattern

Each different type of line included in your design will test your control of the pyrography pen. Remember to select different nibs if you need to, and adjust the temperature, angle, pressure, and speed that you work with accordingly to achieve the required results. This exercise is a good time to test the ways you use a range of different nibs: in my example, I used a skew, a spoon point nib, and a ball stylus writing nib to create a range of lines and marks. Try out some of the different types of marks you

I used a medium skew to form the straight lines on the blank. I used two parallel strokes of the nib to make some of the lines slightly thicker.

I used the fine edge of a spoon point to draw the curved lines of the circle, as this can easily be moved across the surface without catching.

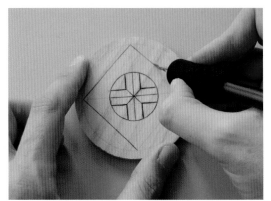

I used the skew to complete the long straight lines, making the most of the sharp edge of the nib to lightly cut across the surface in a smooth motion.

discovered while working through Chapter 1. Curves, straight defined lines, dappled lines with undefined edges, dotted lines, and more are possible—put yourself through your paces.

Decide which line of the design you will complete first. Set the pyrography machine up next to you. Ensure you have enough room to work comfortably. Turn the pyrography machine on and test the nib on a scrap piece of wood if you wish. Hold the coaster and move the heated nib smoothly across the surface, trying to keep

the lines free of errors. If a line is too light, go over it carefully until you achieve the required result. Turn the wooden item around whenever necessary so that your hand moves in the direction needed to complete the line without restriction. Work on each separate line one at a time, completing one before moving onto the next so that you do not make a mistake or use the wrong mark. Your design and choice of line can change or adapt as you work if you feel the balance or structure is not right.

If you wish, you can make each of your coasters identical so that you make a set. Making identical items is a good way to develop your confidence, as you will need to concentrate on achieving the same result every time. However, you can make each coaster slightly different in some way (by keeping the same layout but changing the marks used, for example), or make every coaster completely different: the choice is yours.

Once you have worked your way through some of the other exercises in the book, you may wish to come back to making coasters to use some of the other techniques in your designs. You may decide that you want to add a small handwritten word to the design: written words can be regarded basically as a complicated line with many different changes of direction. The use of lettering is covered in more detail later in the book.

Using the soft edge of a spoon point nib can add a dappled soft line.

Repeatedly applying a ball-point stylus forms a line comprised of many small dots.

Detail was added with some fine broken lines by lightly drawing the point of the skew along the surface, parallel to some of the earlier marks.

Chapter 2

Basic Decoration Techniques

The simplest way to build up your confidence with pyrography is to focus on simple decorative techniques. Basic decoration consists of the repetition of simple marks (such as the ones you practiced in the previous chapter). By repeating basic marks in different combinations and arrangements, it is possible to create borders, tones, shading, and simple designs. In this chapter, we will build on the mark-making exercises we explored in the previous chapter and project. By the end of this chapter, you will have a better understanding of how you can begin decorating objects using simple techniques.

A set of wooden napkin rings, decorated with simple daisy designs and patterned borders.

Branding

In essence, the pyrography pen is no different than a pen or pencil. It is used to create a mark on a surface by adding something to it. The only difference is the pyrography machine applies heat to change the surface rather than an ink or colored pigment. Any technique that can be created using a pen or pencil can be reproduced using a pyrography machine. However, the pyrography pen has a quality pens and pencils don't—its nib profile can be shaped into an almost endless array of shapes. This makes it possible to create a pattern simply by pressing the nib onto the wood like a brand. The most common form of decoration can be found through the use of simple repeated forms. When combined, these form a pattern that can be extremely pleasing to the eye through the visual rhythm it creates. Repeating a design around the outside of an object creates a frame, which can turn a well-drawn image into a successful design with very little effort, making them ideal for beginners in the art of pyrography. Creating a repeating pattern border is a useful technique for simply decorating picture frames and other objects. The principle of using a shaped nib to make a repeating stamped design can also be applied to the entire surface of an object.

As we discussed in Chapter 1, the hot wire machine is particularly versatile due to the freedom provided with the nibs available. With such a range of shaped nibs on the market, a massive scope of potential is open to the crafter simply by pressing a heated nib into a wooden surface. Each different shape puts a different imprint in the wood, and forms a pattern if repeated. Add to that the qualities that can be changed by adjusting temperature, pressure, angle, speed, and contact time with each nib, and the possibilities are literally endless (see sidebars at right).

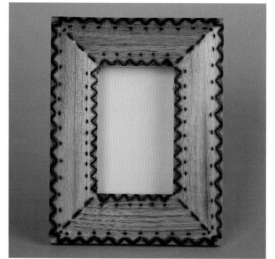

This oak frame was decorated using a wire nib shaped into a V. It was used on a high temperature at regular intervals to create a primitive "stitched" appearance.

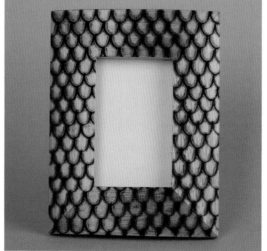

This oak frame is an experiment from my early days in pyrography. I formed a U shape with a wire nib and applied it in rows along the wood to give the effect of scales. You can purchase specialist nibs that create this effect to a very detailed standard.

Spoon Point (bowl)	Spear	Wire Nib
Chisel		Medium Skew (edge)
Medium Skew (face)		Small Circle Shader
Ball Stylus		Circle Stamper
Circle Shader	Large Skew	Spear Shader

Here are some of the different borders that are possible using a number of shaped pyrography nibs.

EXPERIMENT: TEMPERATURE AND CONTACT TIME

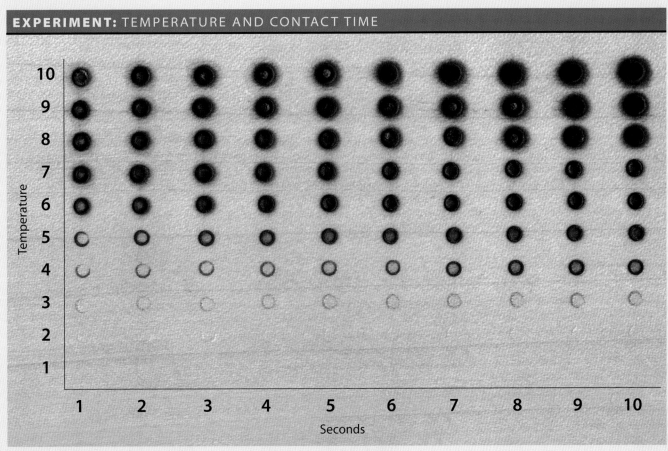

This experiment shows the effects of temperature and the time the nib spent in contact with the wood. I used a circle stamper at different temperatures to press for various lengths of time. The numbers shown along the left side indicate the temperature setting used for each impression. The higher the number, the more obvious the mark made. The numbers shown along the bottom indicate the number of seconds the nib was held against the wood.

EXPERIMENT: SPACING AND ANGLE

The result of experiments with a small spear nib to show the range of borders possible if you alter the spacing, angle, and regularity of the way you apply the nib to the wood.

Photograph courtesy of Razertip.

Borders

One technique I use to create a simple decorative pattern is to press a nib along the edge of a wooden item to create a border. Using the nib to do this in one motion ensures the pattern is regular, and takes less time than drawing a border freehand. The only limit to this is your imagination in shaping the wire nib: I have created semi-circles, shallow curves, triangles, and a range of other shapes in this way. Every specialist nib also has its own unique profile and shape, which can be used for decorative purposes in a massive number of different ways. Using a border such as this can finish off a design nicely. Sometimes it just ties the design into the piece you have been working on by adding a framed effect. With time, you will recognize which designs and scales benefit from the inclusion of such a technique.

Once you have selected your nib, think about how you intend to apply it to the wood. There are literally countless ways you can construct patterned borders once you start practicing, and they can be applied to almost any object or item. Here are some items to consider while planning your stamped design.

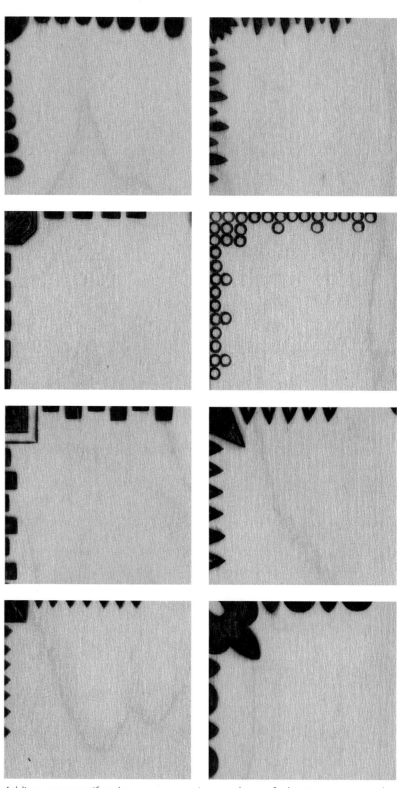

Adding a new motif or shape at a corner is a good way of adapting to a required change of direction.

Adding a decorative border can really finish a design off by framing it. Images can look lost without it.

Gaps

Will each section of pattern directly touch the previous one without gaps? This is probably the easiest way to work if you are just beginning. Or, if you want to leave a regular space between each place where the hot nib is applied, you can consider using a measuring tool as you work along the edge, or perhaps you can mark out each point on the wood lightly with a pencil before you start burning.

DRAGGING: Step by Step

Press a looped wire nib into the edge of the wooden item.

Pull the nib back across the wooden surface toward the edge.

Repeat this all the way around the required area to decorate, creating a simple scalloped border.

Contact time

Take your time as you work along the edge of the wood, making sure you apply the nib in the same way on every occasion. Remember, if you leave the nib on the wood for different periods of time, the marks will vary in tone due to the amount of burning taking place.

Changes in direction

Consider how you will deal with corners or other features of the wooden edge that may affect the pattern. You may need to use a different shape at the corners, or use the nib at a different angle to cope with the change in direction.

Dragging

Once you have started to master making patterned borders by pressing the nib repeatedly into the wood in a single motion, you may wish to consider moving the nib to change the mark that is made. For example, I created a very effective scalloped edge on a decorative plate by shaping the nib into an oval form. I pressed this down onto the wood and then dragged it back toward the edge, filling in the oval form with a smooth darker area of tone.

Basic motifs

While you were experimenting with making your first marks using a pyrography pen, you probably built up a large number of sample marks on scrap pieces of wood—a catalog of experiments for future reference, as I described in the first chapter. Looking back over a vast array of lines, curves, and other marks may spark off inspiration: perhaps a certain mark reminds you of something?

For example, in my initial experiments, I made a series of short marks on a piece of wood with a long pen nib I made from a section of pyrography wire. I used the nib at a medium to high temperature and pressed the length of the wire into the wood at quite a shallow angle. As most of the wire along one side of the nib was in contact with the wood, this resulted in a dark line that gradually tapered into a finer point. This shape reminded me of the delicate petals of a daisy. I drew a small dark circle and proceeded to recreate those marks radiating out from the circle. This created a very simple flower motif I have used in many designs, from key rings and napkin rings to photo frames. Combining marks and lines to form basic motifs is the next stage in the progression of a pyrographer. Go back over some of your previous experiments and start to use them to make small shapes or patterns. Perhaps a certain triangular mark that you made can be combined with four more to make a star? One semi-circular mark on its own may not appear to be significant visually, but it suddenly becomes the scales of a snake or fish when repeated in several rows.

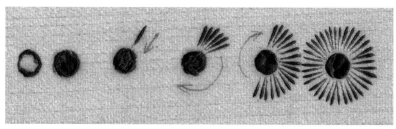

The process for creating a simple daisy motif: Start by making a dark circle and then work your way around, flicking the nib towards the center to create a mark that fades to a narrow point.

A photo frame is a great object to decorate with repeated daisy designs.

You can create a very simple star by applying a spear shader nib against a wooden surface five times at different angles. The finished outline can then be shaded to make a solid form.

Tone and Shade

Once you feel confident with making basic marks and lines, the next stage to consider is using tone and shade. If you have worked with pencil or pen, you will find the principles are basically the same.

Successful shading requires patience, time, a good eye, and a steady hand. Consider how the tone needs to change over the area in question before you start shading: does the tone simply go from light to dark in one direction or does it fluctuate in certain areas? The aim will be to create a smooth area of shading that blends together without appearing uneven, lined, or blotchy. It is best to practice shading on a scrap piece of wood to build up your confidence.

Each different style of nib has its own benefits and drawbacks when it comes to shading. Generally the wider nibs, such as spoon points or similar, are more suitable for shading. The marks they create are softer and broader, making them ideal for covering areas of tone.

You will find the surface of the wood will affect the way in which you shade it in exactly the same way it causes problems trying to make consistent lines and marks. You may need to spend longer burning one difficult area of wood in order to achieve the same tone that only took a matter of seconds nearby.

I've suggested a few exercises here to give you experience creating shaded areas of tone while building up your confidence and sensitivity to the way a pyrography machine works on a wooden surface (see page 52).

Applying tone in different ways

The following two exercises cover using the pyrography pen in either small circular motions or in parallel lines. There are many other shading techniques suitable for use with pyrography. Use of smaller, more random marks or lines can be suitable for creating effects such as fur or hair.

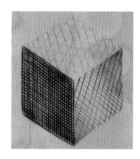

Cross-hatching is a simple way to shade an object. Vary the density and quantity of the lines to create different levels of tone.

Stippling (or pointillism) is a very effective method for shading with pyrography. As with cross-hatching, different degrees of shadow are created by changing the frequency, closeness, and tone of the dots.

Cross-hatching lines is also a good tonal technique, as you can easily vary the angle, thickness, frequency, and density of the lines to create an almost infinite range of tones.

Stippling or pointillism, shading through use of dots, is one of my favorite techniques. It is a very simple, yet effective technique, created by repeatedly dabbing the nib. It can take a long time to cover a larger area of tone, but the soft delicate shaded effect is very versatile and ideal for a range of purposes such as fabric, fur, or other soft materials. Use of very dark dots packed densely over an area creates the darker tones possible, while lighter dots more widely spread over the surface is used to portray the paler shades. Stippling can be done using any nib.

The key points to remember when creating tone, shade, and other basic decoration techniques are patience, sensitivity, and time. Working in pyrography can be a very labor-intensive process, especially when working on larger or complex designs, but the effects can be stunning when you put the effort into the work and do not rush yourself.

PRACTICE EXERCISE: FLAT TONE

To start with, we will look at creating areas of flat tone or shading. You'll create a series of nine boxes that starts with the dark end of the spectrum and finishes with the light. Doing this will begin developing your shading skills. Spoon point nibs are ideal for shading as the soft underside of the bowl is perfect for covering an area with tone without making a sharp edge or line, but it is not essential to use them for this exercise. Just make sure you are comfortable using whatever nib you select.

If you change tone in steps that are too big, you will end up with empty squares. If you do not change the tone sufficiently for each square, you will find that you need extra squares! The aim is to try to get a feel for creating each tone, as well as increasing your visual ability to identify the changes in each tonal value. Hopefully, you will reach the fifth square in the middle where you will be able to create a middle 50% tone that completes the even transition from light to dark.

Draw out your row of 9 squares in pencil on a spare piece of wood. Ideally they should be around ½–1" (15–25mm) in size.

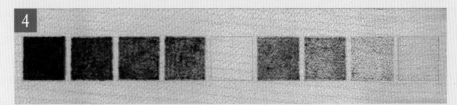

Turn your pyrography machine to high. Using the bowl of the spoon point in small circular motions, fill in the left square so you are left with a dark, almost black, area of tone. Turn off the machine and let it cool.

Shade the square at the opposite end of the row as lightly as possible to create a very pale shade. The square should only be slightly darker than the surrounding unburned wood. Do not pause or press on the surface.

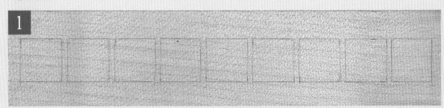

Work your way toward the middle from each end. The first step is to create a tone slightly lighter than the black square, and marginally darker than the palest square. This will allow you to gauge how you are progressing as you work toward the middle tone.

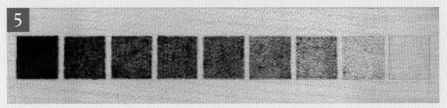

The last remaining square should be the "mid-tone," exactly halfway between the two extremes of shade that you have created.

PRACTICE EXERCISE: GRADUAL TONE CHANGE

The next stage to consider is mastering the technique of changing tone gradually with no apparent inconsistencies or blotches. This can be a particularly difficult skill to master, especially when working with the unpredictable surface qualities of wood.

Draw out a long and narrow rectangle in pencil on your piece of scrap wood and try to shade the box from one end to another, so that one end is almost plain wood and the other is very dark. The aim will be to make the transition as seamless as possible. My main tip would be to start with the lightest tone: it is always easier in pyrography to correct an area that is too light rather than one that has been burned too much and is too dark as a result. It is possible to start at the darkest tone first, but you may find it is harder to control the rate of the tonal change this way. This could leave you with insufficient space to reach the lightest tones for shading: this could make your picture unnecessarily dark without the required contrast of highlights for detail. Some images, such as portraits of people, rely heavily on the softer tones to recreate the appearance of skin, so it is best to adopt a technique that allows you to be as flexible as possible.

Make sure you have cleaned any carbon or grit from the nib so that nothing causes the nib to stick as you shade. Try not to lift the nib off the surface unnecessarily as this will allow the pen to heat up quickly and may cause it to heat the surface too much

Draw a long, thin rectangle on a spare piece of wood approximately ½" high by 4¾" long (15mm high by 120mm long).

Start by shading the full length of the box with a very slight tone, which should only just alter the surface color of the wood.

Leave an area at one side untouched and start to shade the next level of tone. If an area is still too light after you have covered it initially, go back over it carefully to match it in with the correct surrounding areas.

when it is reapplied. Try to keep a steady rhythm across the surface to keep the tone even, and make sure you do not stop in one place too long as this will scorch the surface. If you are not happy with the way the shading is blended, you can always re-work an area to ensure the tonal change is as smooth as possible. It is not an easy process and may take several attempts to get the desired effect.

When completed, you should have a rectangle of tone that shows a change of tone from light through to dark as smoothly as possible. You can carry this activity out as many times as you wish until you feel comfortable with the technique. You can also adapt the exercise slightly to test your own skill and ability: try going evenly from light to dark and back to light again over a defined area, or from dark to light and back to dark. Try to reproduce the smooth shading in a circle to give the effect of a three-dimensional sphere, or shade a more complicated geometric shape to practice working with tone. Each of these activities will give you the opportunity to practice smoothly and seamlessly blending layers of tone, which will aid you enormously when you move onto the more advanced techniques in the later stages of this book.

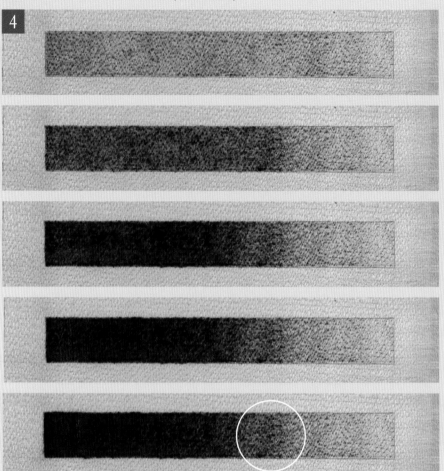

4

Work back over the wood again to repeat this process. You may need to increase the heat of the nib slightly at each stage, or just work over the surface slightly longer, depending on the nib you have chosen and the type of machine you are using. I have 7 tonal shifts in my example.

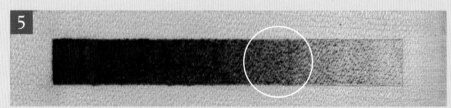

5

Keep an eye open for inconsistencies. If an area does not appear to be dark enough on your initial attempt, then feel free to go back over it lightly to correct it. If you do make an area too dark, it may be possible to correct it by lightly rubbing it with fine sandpaper or the edge of a craft knife.

Key rings are one of my favorite items to create. I have created literally dozens of designs for sale at craft fairs and as commissions for customers. They are popular items because they will be used on a regular basis: everyone will take hold of their keys at least once a day! Because of their size, they are relatively quick to complete and can be as detailed or as simple as you like. I usually have dozens of blank fobs in my supplies so that I can work on them whenever the mood takes me. You can use them to test out ideas for larger designs, or just let your imagination run wild and see what the results are. They are also easy to replicate, so you can make any number of identical designs if a certain image proves particularly popular with your friends and family.

The aim of this exercise is to take some of the basic decoration techniques discussed so far and use them to form a simple design. We'll put the information you read in Chapter 2 to good use, as well as building on the lessons you learned from Chapter 1 and the project you completed there. The benefit of using a small surface such as a key ring fob is that your focus is on the techniques rather than arranging a complicated layout. To give you an idea of how many different possibilities there are when working on key rings, I've included pictures of three designs that I completed with a range of decorations on them.

Key rings are great fun to work on and the potential range of designs is only restricted by your imagination.

TOOLS & MATERIALS

- Blank key ring fob of choice
- Pencil
- Pyrography machine
- Pyrography nibs of choice

1. Preparation

For this project, you will need nothing more than some blank key ring fobs, your pyrography machine, and your imagination! I would recommend you use a pencil to draw the designs first, but you can always try working straight onto the wood with the pyrography pen once you feel confident doing so.

Many craft suppliers will sell shaped wooden fob blanks in packs, pre-drilled and with the metal rings included in the price. They can usually be found in a variety of shapes. You may also wish to work on leather key ring fobs, as they are equally easy to find at a reasonable price: just remember to ensure the blanks are made of vegetable-tanned leather so you do not subject yourself to any horrid fumes as you work.

We'll use three design elements in the project to build on the linear work we did in Project 1. The three elements are: drawing a simple motif (or an arrangement of motifs), some basic shading, and a patterned border or edging. I'll take you through the process for three of my designs. Feel free to use these designs for practice or to apply the principles you learn from them to your own images and designs.

Remember to be careful when working on small items such as key ring fobs. Your fingers will inevitably be closer to the hot nib of the pyrography machine, so try to make sure you do not inadvertently burn yourself while working.

Wooden key ring blanks can be purchased in a variety of shapes.

2. Draw Lines

Here are the completed line drawings. The outlines for each design were drawn onto the blanks carefully using a fine-bladed nib.

The first thing you must do is to select a design to draw. Draw it onto the wood in pencil first. If you have a range of different fob shapes, try to select an image that fits the shape well and fills the available space. The following drawings show the step-by-step method for constructing a few basic images: these are ideal for small designs such as key rings. These ideas are meant as suggestions if you need inspiration or a starting point for this project. I used a range of shaped fobs that are commonly available. Each should be approached carefully when you want to plan a design's layout: a circular motif can look small or lost on a long, narrow fob, for example.

Select an appropriate nib for burning the lines of your image into the wood. The edge of a spoon point nib is suitable, as are most writing nibs. Make sure you are holding the wooden fob firmly, as it can be easy to slip when working on small items if the nib catches or snags on the surface. Take your time and try to ensure the lines are as fine and smooth as possible, using a medium heat setting and going over the line to smooth it out or fill any gaps if necessary. Try to make sure the lines stop where they meet and do not cross over unnecessarily, as this will help you to develop your control in using the pen.

DRAWING A ROSE: Step by Step

This is the basic way to draw a simplified rose design. Start with a small circle (A) and draw two or three curved lines inside (B). It is then just a matter of slowly working outward with a series of curved lines to form the rings of petals: four or five rings are sufficient (C, D, E). If you want and if you have the room, you can also add a couple of leaf shapes at the base of the flower, with some lines to represent the veins (F).

    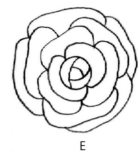 

A   B   C   D   E   F

DRAWING A BUTTERFLY: Step by Step

Butterflies are another image that can be drawn very easily. Start with two small ovals that touch at one end (A). Add two lines with dots on the end for the antennae (B). Add the wings next: these should be as symmetrical as possible if you draw them freehand (C). If this causes problems, you could draw the wings on one side and then trace them to recreate them identically on the opposite side (D). You can then draw some patterns or markings inside the wings to add interest (E), or some stripes across the body (F).

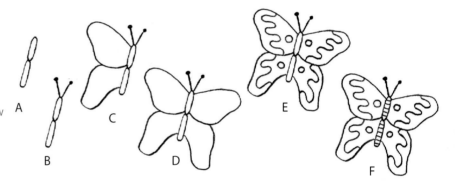

DRAWING A CHICKEN: Step by Step

I have used a cartoon chicken design on a number of occasions in my pyrography work. Start with a loose triangular shape: the points do not have to be sharp and the lines do not have to be straight (A). Add a triangular beak and the comb on the head (B). Draw a row of arcs across the neck area to define the head and add a circular eye (C). Draw two lines on for the wings (D) and add the feet (E). Finally add the last details to the beak, eyes, and anywhere else that you want (F)!

3. Shade

Once you have completed the lines of the drawn image, plan how you will add some shading or tone to the image to make it a little more substantial. During this time, your pyrography machine can be switched off and allowed to cool down, so you can change to a shading nib if you wish. I have used a different shading technique on each of my three sample designs to show you a range of options and methods available.

SHADING THE ROSE: Step by Step

For the rose, I used a partial shading technique, adding tone to help define the different areas and enhance the impression of the image in three dimensions. This was completed using a shading nib on a low temperature to slightly darken along some lines and create a sense of shadow (A). I went over the shading again on the leaves to darken them and make them appear as though they are behind the rose (B).

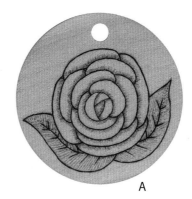

A   B

SHADING THE BUTTERFLY: Step by Step

For the butterfly design, I drew a pattern of spots and markings across the wings and shaded each area smoothly using two different tones. I used the bowl of a spoon point nib in a smooth motion over the surface to create each tone, working carefully between the lines to keep the shading even and consistent (A, B). I finished by alternately shading the striped body of the butterfly using a higher temperature setting to make them appear black in color (C).

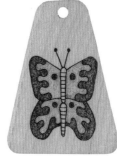

A   B   C

SHADING THE CHICKEN: Step by Step

The chicken was shaded using a more textural approach. I used the soft side of the spoon point bowl to shade the chicken, dabbing the bowl onto the body repeatedly to give a soft appearance resembling the feathers. I did this loosely all over the chicken body to create a general texture (A), and then built up the intensity of the dots in some areas to give them impression of shadow (B). I added some short lines on the head for a contrasting texture, and then added some smooth tone to the legs, beak, and comb. The eye was shaded very darkly using a higher temperature in one touch of the pyrography nib (C).

A   B   C

4. Create a border

The final stage is to add a patterned border or edge. This finishes off your design by framing it on the wood. The most simple and effective way to do this is by using a shaped nib you apply to the wood at regular intervals. Any nib will have a number of ways you can apply it to make a different effect, or you may wish to shape your own nib if you have a specific idea in mind.

Use a scrap piece of wood to practice your border on before you apply it to the key ring fob. You will need to make sure the temperature setting is correct for the effect you want to achieve. A high setting may result in scorching or lines that are not clear enough. Similarly, the lines may be broken or faint if the machine's temperature dial is set too low. Consider the way you hold and apply an existing nib, or make your own shaped nib using a short length of dichrome wire and a pair of pliers. When you have decided on the style you want to use, work your way around the edge of the fob, making each mark as evenly and consistently as possible so that the pattern is formed.

Once the fob is finished, simply thread the metal ring through the hole and it is ready to be attached to your keys. Because key ring blanks are very affordable and quick to decorate, you can create dozens of designs in no time at all and with very little financial outlay.

CREATING BORDERS: Step by Step

I used a different nib for each key ring to show some different possible patterns for the borders. I used the tip of a spear nib on the chicken fob to create a zigzag of small triangles (A). I used a ball stylus point to make the border on the rose fob, leaving small gaps between each spot (B). On the butterfly key ring, I used a chisel-shaped nib to leave rectangular marks around the edge at regular intervals (C). Each border was made with the next mark in sequence almost touching the last, but you can also spread them apart with more space in between if you prefer.

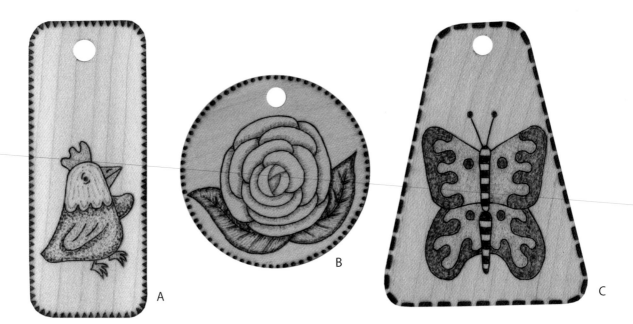

A

B

C

Chapter 3

Silhouettes

The art of pyrography is characterized by the process of making

dark marks on a lighter surface, which makes the technique ideal

for the creation and depiction of silhouettes. As a silhouette is

generally created using only two tones, they are an ideal starting

point for someone starting out in pyrography—the results can

be stunning despite their simplicity.

This basswood box lid
was decorated with
the silhouette of a stag
against the countryside,
surrounded by a simple
border to frame the image.

About Silhouettes

A silhouette is generally a dark shadow or outline against the contrast of a light background, or vice versa. Most silhouettes are black against a white background, though in photography, silhouettes are created when an object is positioned in front of a bright light. Traditionally, silhouettes were used to create portraits by cutting and shaping black card as far back as the eighteenth century. The visual impact of silhouettes has continued into the modern era, and it can still be seen today used in areas as diverse as graphic design, advertising, and the movie industry. A simple silhouette can make a dramatic impact when used correctly, and they can be immediately recognizable despite the lack of detail other than an outline. The Statue of Liberty, the Sydney Opera House, the Eiffel Tower, the Pyramids of Giza—all of these famous places have been represented and photographed as silhouettes.

This rustic wooden pot was decorated with a series of cacti silhouettes, completed with a Mexican sunburst motif on the lid.

Many graphic silhouettes of famous people have gone on to become iconic images in their own right, reproduced innumerable times on T-shirts and posters. A few famous examples include Alfred Hitchcock, James Bond, and the recent iPod advertising campaign.

Silhouettes—profiles cut from black paper—were a popular method of portraiture during the 18th century.

The benefit of using silhouettes in pyrography is you can create a striking image just by burning a detailed outline and filling it with tone. Silhouettes make a good subject for crafters starting out in pyrography (and for you at this point in the book) because they build on your mark-making skills to create the outline and your shading ability to create large areas of solid dark tone, all while keeping to the detailed outline you have created. It's just like learning to color inside the lines when you were starting at your first school!

This photograph of the Pyramids of Giza demonstrates another way to capture a silhouette.

Subjects for Silhouettes

Silhouettes can be used to create images in a range of subjects and themes. As previously discussed, silhouettes were originally used to represent people, and can still be used as such. Animals, objects, landmarks, and many other famous or typical subjects can be found using the Internet, your camera, and your imagination. Inspiration for your silhouette designs can be found in many places. Keep your eyes open for unexpected opportunities, particularly when looking at natural forms.

People

It is very easy to use basic silhouettes to portray people, but there are a number of factors to bear in mind. Portraits work very well in profile so you can see distinguishing features such as the shape of the nose, forehead, chin, and other facial features. Portraits where the subject is face-on may not be as successful unless the person has a particularly distinctive hairstyle, as the facial features will not be apparent.

Animals

Animals make great subjects for silhouette designs, as their body shapes are often easily distinguishable from the outline alone. Many animals have features that look nice when applied in a silhouette, such as the antlers of a stag, the trunk and tusks of an elephant, or the long neck of the giraffe. You can also incorporate some landscape features into the silhouette in order to represent the natural habitat of the animal concerned, which makes a really successful image. Animals can be drawn freehand if you feel able, but there is a range of other pictorial sources for inspiration available if you need assistance: these include photographs, books, magazines, and the Internet.

Landscapes

Landscapes can also be used for inspiration when creating silhouette designs. It is very simple to make a landscape design, which can be viewed at its most simplistic as a dark shaped band across a pale background. Inspiration for landscape designs can come from the area where you live,

Many landmarks are famed for the imposing and significant profiles that they create, such as the Statue of Liberty.

Landscapes are an excellent subject for silhouette designs as they are often instantly recognizable, such as this design based on the profile of Stonehenge in Wiltshire.

Animal silhouettes are very simple and extremely effective.

or from somewhere further away which inspires you or is symbolic to you for personal reasons.

Landscapes can be used to create senses of mood. Even generic landscapes can be used to create very emotive silhouette designs. A delicate design incorporating rolling hills and windblown trees will create a calming and peaceful ambience, while a dramatic cityscape depicting distinctive examples of modern architecture may give a feeling of activity and energy. A desolate scene of crumbling ruins in an old cemetery may instill a feeling of loss, sadness, or nostalgia in the eyes of the viewer.

The subject material for landscape designs is almost limitless. There are many buildings and skylines all around the world that are instantly recognizable due to their shape and features. You may be able to use your own photographs from your travels to provide you with the raw materials to trace or draw a design from. You do not have to be bound by the limits of the visual sources either: you can create your own personal landscape by combining parts from several images. Why not have the Statue of Liberty alongside Big Ben and the Sphinx if you wish? Use your imagination to create a design that is rich in creativity and personal to you. You may wish to create fantasy landscapes if your imagination takes you that way. Silhouettes of dramatic space cities, medieval towns, and prehistoric vistas are only a thought away.

From Inspiration to Pattern

Now that you have some ideas of where to find subjects to create in silhouette, you need to know how to get those ideas into a form that you can transfer into wood and pyrography form. There are several ways to do this.

Photographs

Photographs or other two-dimensional images are the most common sources of silhouttes. As the image has already been transferred into a flat design, it is very easy to use such sources for the basis of a silhouette design. You can simply trace the required outline from the source, or trace and combine sections from different photographs to make a new design. When using a photograph

I used the digital effects on my computer to break this photograph down into a limited number of tones.

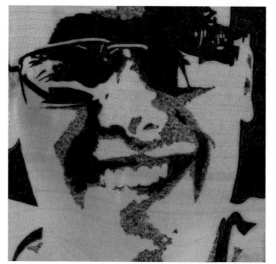

The computer manipulation was then used to form this pyrography silhouette design with a mid-tone to add extra contrast and detail.

or other flat image as the basis for a silhouette design, your first concern should be matching the size of the source material to the required size of the item to be decorated. If the design is too large, it will lack in detail and interest. If the design is too small, it will lack impact and may look lost on the decorated item. You can use a photocopier or the image manipulation software on your computer to enlarge or reduce a photograph prior to tracing.

If desired, you can also use computer software to manipulate a digital photo into a state that's much easier to translate into pyrography. By increasing the contrast of a photo, you force the computer to decide whether an area is light or dark—thereby cutting out any decision making for yourself.

Drawing

Drawing is a great way to create your own silhouettes in freehand directly onto the surface you intend to decorate. The only limit in this way is your imagination and your artistic ability.

Shadow drawing

Shadow drawing is a good way to grab interesting shadows that crop up on you unexpectedly. I was in my garden one summer when I observed the shadow cast by a twisted willow tree on a nearby wall. The detail of each delicately gnarled branch and delicate leaf was very clear due to the strong sunlight. I placed a piece of white paper behind the tree and was able to carefully trace an area of the shadow for use as a potential design in the future. You have to be careful where you place your hand while working so you don't accidentally block the sunlight and obscure the shadow, but the results can be very exciting if you are patient. You can recreate this form of shadow drawing using a strong lamp to cast a shadow from any object onto a piece of paper or perhaps directly onto a piece of wood.

Shadows can be great sources of silhouette designs. Keep large pieces of white paper, pencils, and a bright light on hand and you'll be able to take advantage of this technique.

PRACTICE EXERCISE: SIMPLE SILHOUETTES

Before starting on your first silhouettes in pyrography, you may wish to carry out a few practical exercises. The simplest way to build your confidence is to draw out some basic shapes in pencil on some scrap pieces of wood, burn in their outlines, and then shade them. Try to use shapes that are complex and will test you both when working on the outline and the shading. Shapes with combinations of straight, curved, and irregular edges will test your ability to draw regular and even edges for the outline. Stars are a good shape to practice on as they have narrow points that require care when shading between the lines, as well as broader areas of tone for coverage.

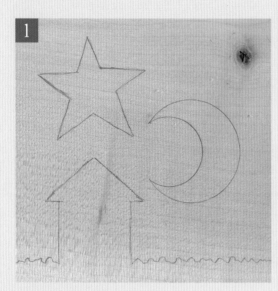

Draw a selection of simple shapes. Make sure to include a range of features to test your abilities, such as curved lines and sharp points.

Use a bladed or similar nib to create the outline of each shape as carefully as you can.

Use a spoon point or similar nib to create a protective border along the inside of each outline, working away from the line into the area to be shaded.

Use the bowl of the spoon point nib to block in the remaining areas, using a constant motion across the surface to make the tone as even as possible.

Considerations for Pyrography Silhouettes

The flowing figure of this wooden platter reminded me of a cloudy sky, so I added a simple landscape based on a photograph taken across a canal in Venice.

This miniature wooden treasure chest is decorated with light-on-dark silhouetted patterns and motifs.

I added a series of deer silhouettes to each side of this box, tracing the animal profiles from a range of different photographs and sources.

There are many considerations to keep in mind when designing a pyrography silhouette. The figure of the wood you're working on, the shape of the object, the size of the pattern—all of these items influence the final product.

Work with the wood

Careful planning and placement of the design on the wood may give you additional benefits or features that could not be reproduced. The character of the wood will add an extra dimension to your design and can be used sensitively to supplement and enhance work you have created. An intricate knot may give the effect of an ominous stormy sky, while the softer figure of a paler wood may provide a watery effect for a seascape. An item that many may disregard as flawed or imperfect may actually be the perfect inspiration for a unique design that would not have arisen without the perception of the artist in that particular place at that moment in time. If you have a plain piece of wood or a blank stock object, you may wish to utilize a light silhouette on a dark background.

Layout

Working on a flat sheet of wood can be like working on a piece of paper or canvas, in that your design will simply stop when you reach the edge of the surface. When you are working on three-dimensional objects, you will need to consider what happens to the silhouette when it reaches an edge or corner. Does the silhouette continue on the new plane or side, and does this affect the way that the design is positioned or laid out? If the design is to be limited to a particular side of an object, I often combine the silhouette with a simple geometric border to frame it, which can be particularly effective on items such as box lids.

Creating a Pyrography Silhouette

Creating a silhouette with pyrography has several distinct steps. I'll describe them below. Follow along as I burn a scene from a photograph I took in Venice, Italy.

I selected this photograph I took on a trip to Venice to use as the basis for a silhouette design.

Planning the outline

Once you have chosen the subject or source of inspiration for a silhouette design, you need to start by creating the outline of the silhouette. You will need to mark up the outline on the wooden surface. You can do this by drawing it freehand or tracing it for transfer to the wood.

Planning the highlights

Another technique to bring more definition and detail to your silhouettes is to use highlights. These areas may be used to pick out features of your design. For example, when creating a cityscape of black shadows against a white background, why not lay out windows in white to add more definition to the shape of the dark building? When you start to add detail in the form of highlights, you are simply increasing the number of outlines in the design. Another benefit of adding highlights or layers to your silhouette design is the three-dimensional effect it gives to an otherwise flat graphic image.

If you do wish to use more definition in creating your silhouette design when working from a photograph or similar, I use this simple guideline to help me work out what areas should be dark and which should remain light to create highlights. Look at the image you are working from and try to break it down visually into areas of tone. Very dark areas will obviously become the shadow in your design, while paler areas will form the light contrast. The difficult areas to classify are the colors and mid-tones. I tend to look at these areas and pick a tone that falls in the middle. Any areas that are darker than my mid-tone will be treated as part of the shadow area, whereas any areas lighter than my mid-tone form the lighter section.

When adding highlights to your design, I recommend shading dark areas with your pencil so there isn't any confusion when you burn the pattern.

You may wish to use software to change a color image to black and white, as it can be easier to break the image down when you are considering different shades of grey rather than colors.

Trace the basic details where there is a dramatic change in tone. Add highlights by splitting the mid-tones into light and dark.

Burning the outline

You will need to choose an appropriate nib for the outline. Consider the qualities of the line first so you make the correct choice. If there are lots of intricate shapes and sharp changes of direction required, you may wish to use a writing nib or the edge of a spoon point so that you can readily change direction. It is possible to use a bladed nib because they are ideal for creating sharp and crisp lines, but you will have to be prepared to move the item around a lot and create the line in sections. Bladed nibs are not as well suited to sharp changes in direction, because they operate by sinking down into the wooden surface slightly. Trying to turn them suddenly can damage the surface of the item you are working on.

The best temperature for creating the outline is generally a medium to high setting. It needs to be hot enough to create a distinct dark outline for the edge of the shaded area. If the outline is too light or insignificant, the edge will only become defined when you start to shade it in. This can lead to a softer or less distinct effect. If the temperature is set too high when you create the outline, then the line may become blobbed or scorched in places where you slow down to create detail. The quality of the silhouette outline is essential, so don't try to cut corners or rush yourself. Remember it is always easier to start light and build the tone up if necessary: time and patience are immensely important in pyrography, as you cannot hurry the work. Dealing with burned or scorched areas takes more time to rectify than simply taking a little extra caution in the first place.

Remember to position the wooden surface so you are moving the pyrography nib naturally across the surface, working with the natural motion of your hand and wrist rather than against it. This will help to ensure you create flowing and even lines with less chance of errors caused through awkward movement or restriction. Turn the wood around frequently so you are always working in a comfortable position. You do not have to keep the wood in one position in front of you.

Preparing to shade

Working with silhouettes can mean you need to shade or block in large areas of dark tone to complete a design. This should not put you off—the effect can be stunning due to the visual impact such designs can provide. If you haven't marked the dark areas with a pencil, do so now.

The main aim when shading large areas of tone for a silhouette is to ensure the color remains as even as possible. This is achieved by being sensitive to the qualities of the wooden item that you are decorating. Many woods, such as birch or sycamore, are even in grain and figure, so the dark tone can readily be applied in a smooth and even way. Other woods with more pronounced grain or other surface features (such as knots) may require more attention: some areas may burn very easily while others take more time and attention to bring them to the required grade of tone. The key point is to be patient and to work at the tone according to the way it responds to the application of the nib.

Once you have transferred the design onto the wooden surface, use a nib of choice to draw the outline of each area.

I often use spoon point nibs when working on silhouette designs because they are versatile. Once I have used the narrow edge of the spoon to create the details and outline, I can then turn the nib over to use the soft bowl side to create the shading. The rounded bowl of the nib travels smoothly over the wooden surface so you can easily cover the surface using small circular motions to leave a smooth dark tone. Alternatively, you can repeatedly press the bowl against the wood in a dabbing motion: this creates a dappled surface that resembles soft leather or fabric.

Broader nibs are the best and most appropriate for shading, as we have discussed in previous chapters. Spoon points are ideal, as are any other wider-shaped specialist nibs. Generally, the broader the nib, the larger the area of tone it will create: this means that you should be able to cover the required surface with the tone with less unnecessary effort than if you were using an unsuitable small nib.

Designs such as this can get quite complex. For ease of reference, I used a pencil to mark the areas that would eventually be shaded.

As silhouettes use a dark tone, the best temperature to use is generally a medium setting at minimum, tending toward the higher end of the temperature gauge. This also assists in heating the larger nibs used for shading to the required temperature. Because the heat is not concentrated over a smaller contact area, you should find that it is still easy to work across the surface without burning it heavily.

When preparing to shade your silhouette, you will need to position the wooden surface or item carefully, in such a way that you are working away from the outline into the area to be shaded. This should prevent the nib from inadvertently burning areas that are to remain plain and ruining the sharp outline. I usually rest my hand on the area that is to be shaded so that the point of the pyrography pen is inside the outline, pointing toward it.

HOMEMADE SHADING NIB

If you do not have access to any specialist shaped nibs designed for shading, it is possible to make an impromptu shading nib out of pyrography wire. Cut a 2⅜" (60mm) length of wire and make a writing nib using the instructions from Chapter 1 (page 32). Once you have fitted the nib into the pyrography pen, pinch the ends together with a pair of pliers so that the section at the end is touching and parallel. Ideally you will have approximately ⅛–³⁄₁₆" (3–5mm) at the writing end that is doubled up. Use the pliers to ensure both sides are flat and not kinked at all. Bend the end of the tip so that as much wire as possible is in contact with the wood when you hold the pen in the burning position. This may take a few attempts to get right, but just keep checking the position and making necessary adjustments with the pliers. In essence, you will have created your own version of a basic spoon or shading point.

Use a small shading nib to create the protective border along the inside edge of each area that will be shaded black.

Protective borders

You will need to be very cautious when working along the outline to prevent damaging the crisp line you are shading within, especially if the line is rich in detail or contains small shapes.

I always use the following process when shading silhouettes. I use a nib, such as a spoon point, to work my way along the edge of the outline itself in order to create a band of shading at least ⅛" (3mm) in width on the side of the line that is to be shaded. The edge of the spoon point can be used for smaller areas of shading, such as inside sharp points or narrow bands of tone. Using the edge in this way ensures you can control the shading in the areas where it is vital not to ruin the outline you have so carefully created.

The ⅛" (3mm) band of tone acts as a protective border, so you can then move on to blocking in the large areas of remaining tone with a broader nib if necessary, safe in the knowledge you no longer have to work next to the outline and risk going over or scorching it. Once the border has been added to every outline, you are left with the simple task of shading in the remaining large blocks of tone in the shaded areas.

The finished protective border has been added to the outlines. You are now ready to start blocking in the largest areas of tone.

Blocking and filling

At this point, you are left with the simplest task of all, which is to create large areas of dark tone—very similar to coloring in with crayons when you were a child! Use the pen in the same way across the area to be shaded so that the marks are uniform. You can work in parallel lines, move the nib in small circular motions, or use a repeated dabbing motion. If you work in the same way at a consistent speed across the whole area, you should prevent any blotchy or uneven patches appearing in the dark tone you are creating. Spend a little more time on the areas that are resistant to burning, and you will have an impressive area of dark tone before you know it.

If you are working on a particularly large silhouette design, you can use a larger shading nib to block and fill the remaining areas once the protective borders have been completed on each outline. The protective border can be used to fill in all of the fine detail, leaving you free to use a larger nib to shade the remaining blocks of tone. You are then able to work at a slightly higher temperature and with the larger nib, safe in the knowledge you do not have to work too close to the detailed outlines you have created.

Use a large shading nib on a medium to high temperature setting to fill in the remaining areas. Keep the pen constantly moving so that the tone is constant without uneven or heavy burning.

The completed silhouette design shows the combination of shadows and highlights to form a single design.

Complex Silhouettes

Once you have completed your first few block silhouettes using two contrasting tones, you can easily move on to more complex or intricate designs. Consider how much detail you wish to go into with your silhouette design. Do you want a simple design, where the features of the design are blocked in completely with the darker color and the background is left as the contrasting white? Or do you wish to add highlights and layers to the landmarks to create more definition and detail? Each approach has its own benefits in terms of appearance and appeal: the most important consideration for any crafter is the more detail, the longer the work will take to complete!

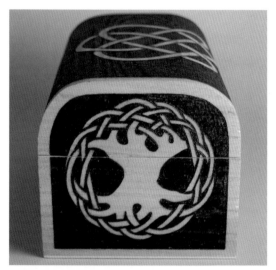

White silhouettes against a black background can be very striking, as this Celtic tree design shows.

This Halloween plate shows the use of layered silhouettes. White silhouettes are used against the main blank landscape to add more interest and detail.

Light on dark

I often create silhouette designs where I use a black background to contrast with the white shapes of the design itself. In essence, this way of working is no different to creating a black shadow against a lighter background, but the finished effect can provide a very different impression that benefits certain designs.

Layers of interest

Another way that I often add more detail to my work in silhouette is to use layers of interest. This is basically a way of adding more interest to a design rather than leaving larger areas blank and even in tone. Imagine you are working on a design where you intend to create a dark landscape of buildings against a pale background. Rather than blocking in the whole foreground with the darker tone, you could add another outline that could become a lighter row of buildings in contrast with the darker ones behind them. Adding foregrounds can bring more depth to your designs, rather than leaving them as bold single silhouettes.

You can add as many layers as you wish to suit the design you are trying to create. Each new layer can contrast with the previous so you constantly swap the tones to add more detail against the last. Black-on-white will become white-on-black, then back to black-on-white again as you continue to work toward or away from the eye of the viewer. This technique can be used to give a frame effect to your designs by shaping the outer edge of the canvas and incorporating it into the design rather than working across it.

With the pressures on our day-to-day routine to be in the right place at the right time, an attractive (and reliable) clock is an essential item in any home. Making your own clock is a great project—you can make the design special and incorporate your own preferences of image and style. In this project, we will use silhouettes to decorate a hanging wall clock, making a bold and attractive design. Silhouette designs are ideal for such items, as the striking design makes a strong visual impact. You can replicate the design I have chosen as a starting point if you wish, but you can also work with any subject matter you feel appropriate.

Clocks are rewarding to work on, and there are no limits to the decorations you can use.

1. Preparation

Wooden clock blanks are widely available for crafters to buy, particularly on the Internet. They are usually sold with a pre-drilled hole for the movement and can be found in a range of sizes and shapes, including round, square, rectangular, octagonal, and many more. The faces can be available in birch plywood, as well as woods such as sycamore or beech. Many suppliers sell kits for the crafter that include an appropriate movement and hands: all you normally need to add is the correct battery.

If the blank face you buy is not supplied with a movement, you can purchase them separately, but you need to ensure the shaft on the movement (which is inserted through a hole in the face so that the hands can be attached) is long enough to cope with the thickness of the wooden face you have chosen. The hands themselves are often available in a range of colors, styles, and finishes, so you are guaranteed to find a set that fits in with your planned design.

2. Select Elements

The first stage is to consider what you want to incorporate in your clock design. Think about the room that the clock is going to be displayed in, or the person who you are making the clock for if it is to be a gift. You may want to create a design with a certain theme in mind, or construct an image that tells a story: this can be a particularly useful approach when creating a clock for a child's bedroom. Carry out research into the sort of images that you would like to use to build up a design. You may find it helpful to look on the Internet, in books or magazines, or to just sketch your own ideas freehand.

For my clock design, I decided to create a woodland theme based on the silhouettes of stags and trees. Both of these subjects can make fascinating and striking designs, especially when they are very intricate in detail. I traced the basic outline of a stag from a photograph, adding some of my own details to make the antlers more impressive. I also found the basic outline of a tree canopy to use in my design.

You can purchase clock craft kits that come complete with the correct movement and hands.

I traced this silhouette of a stag to use as part of the composite design layout.

3. Draw Borders

Once you have decided on the basic elements of your composition, the next step is to draw out any border using a pencil: you may need to use a ruler or a pair of compasses as well if your clock face is a geometric shape. A border can help to frame the silhouettes and finish the design in a more appropriate manner. Decide how you want the border to look. Will you have a straight solid line, or two thinner lines? Will the border be shaped in any way to make it more decorative? I would suggest the border is best kept as simple as possible so the silhouettes form the focus of the design. Remember that the border can reflect the silhouette designs you have chosen if you choose the style and form appropriately.

When planning the border, consider the area the hands will move across as well. If there is too much detail going on under the clock hands, it may make it difficult to tell the time, as the image will distract the eye. This is a particular problem if the hands are black or similar in color to the burned tones underneath. You can get around this problem by either leaving a blank area around the pre-drilled hole, or using clock hands that stand out against the surface: you may be able to buy colored or metallic hands, or paint them yourself.

4. Lay Out the Elements

The layout for the silhouette elements can be drawn onto the wooden clock face once the border has been marked up. Completing the borders first is useful as it helps to define exactly the area in which you will be working. I repeated each main element to make the design symmetrical, and then drew the tree trunk and some grasses freehand to complete the layout.

Keep in mind the area the clock hands will cover as they move around each hour. For this project, you may just choose to position one symbol at the 12 o'clock position, or four symbols to represent the 12, 3, 6, and 9 o'clock points on the face. If you do this, these need to be carefully planned in relationship to the central hole where the hands will radiate from.

In this layout, I have tried to use the negative space in the design to emphasize them. The 12 o'clock position is marked by the blank space between the two trees, while the 6 o'clock position can be seen between the heads of the two stags. The 3 and 9 o'clock positions are marked by the tip of each tallest antler.

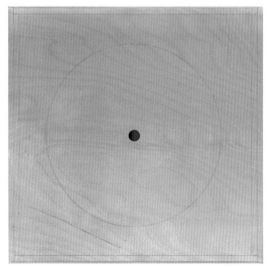

I marked a circle around the pre-drilled hole to show how far the minute hand would reach. I also drew the borders for my design in pencil.

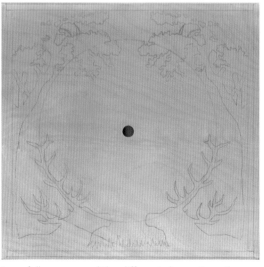

I carefully composed the different elements so they did not stray too far into the area that the hands would move across.

I used a fine bladed nib to carefully draw the borders and outline of the whole design.

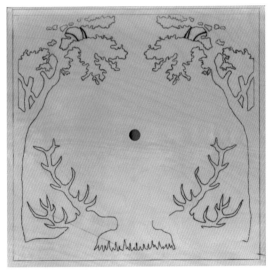

I used a small spoon point nib to fill in the narrowest areas of the design, before moving on to add a protective border inside each different part of the outline.

I then used a larger shading nib to block in the remaining areas of tone. Keep the pen moving in small circular motions to avoid burning the surface.

5. Burn the Outline

Once you have drawn out the entire design in pencil, use a fine nib, such as a blade point or the lip of a spoon nib, to draw the outline of the border's sides. Use a medium heat so you don't scorch the wood and distort the line. Work slowly and carefully to keep the line as even as possible. When the border has been completed, move onto the outlines of the design itself, taking your time to ensure the lines are as crisp and concise as possible with no mistakes.

6. Burn the Protective Edge

When you have completed the outlines, you can start to fill the border lines by shading with an appropriate nib, such as the bowl of a spoon nib. I used a small spoon point nib to create a protective edge just inside each outline to reduce the chance of any mistakes as I filled in the design.

7. Shade and Finish

Once you have completed that step, you can change to a broader shading nib to fill in any remaining areas of the design yet to be blocked in. Try to use a smooth motion as you shade, keeping the nib constantly moving so you do not burn the wood too deeply or unevenly.

When you have finished shading, the clock design should be complete. You can treat the wooden face with Danish oil if you wish, using a soft cloth to rub the oil into the wood. I would recommend a couple of coats, but make sure you let the clock face dry fully between each coat.

You can then assemble the clock movement through the pre-drilled hole. Insert a battery into the compartment. You are now ready to set your clock to the correct time and hang it up on your wall, or perhaps give it to someone as a gift. Time flies when you're having fun with pyrography!

Chapter 4

Drawing with Fire

The most flexible way to create a visual design to be burned

onto an object using pyrography is to draw it freehand. You

may feel that such artistic skills are not your strongest asset, but

don't let that prevent you from enjoying this aspect of the craft.

In essence, the pyrography machine shares most in common

with the pen or pencil above all other art media. Using the point

of the nib creates sharp lines or intricate details, while using it

on a broader side can create areas of shade or tone. Almost any

activity you would find in an instructional drawing book can also

be applied in principle to the pyrography pen.

This decorative wooden
trinket box was adorned
with many different
drawings in line with the
preferences of the girl it
was made for.

Drawing vs. Pyrography

In pyrography, we often try to achieve the neatest line we can on the wooden surface in the same way we would hope to draw a flawless line on a piece of paper. The pyrography machine uses the fickle and unpredictable element of heat to make its mark on a surface that has its own imperfections and irregularities. These variable factors mean the results of applying the heat to the wood can never be guaranteed, and we must remain open to these eventualities when working with pyrography.

Many pyrography books state that a heavy mark that scorches the wood around the line is not desirable or correct. Rather than working with that instruction as a definitive rule to be strictly adhered to, keep yourself open to the possibilities of any mark made. What appears initially as an accident may actually be just the result you hope to achieve at some point in the future when working on another design. You are literally drawing with fire when you use a pyrography machine, so you must bear the consequences in mind.

At the end of the day, no mark is wholly wrong or incorrect in a creative sense. Many of the modern painting techniques we regard so highly today were frowned upon by the peers of the day, but it is this sense of experimentation and openness in the face of new ideas that leads to discovery and creativity. Don't regard what appears to initially be an error as simply that alone: consider it a new and unplanned opportunity for exploration in the future! I remember creating sheet upon sheet of trials, marks, and experiments when working in a new media for the first time at all levels of my studies in art and design. Experimentation is by far the best means to improve your understanding of what the pyrography machine can do and the techniques that it is suited for.

This photo frame was one of my first experimental drawings when I was starting out in pyrography. I used a nib shaped into a small semi-circle to create the texture of the tree canopy.

Use a scrap piece of wood to experiment with what you can achieve with the pyrography machine. You may find that inadvertently holding the pen too long on the wood creates an orange scorched flare around the mark that is not suitable for the fine detailed work you are about to embark on, but it may one day be the perfect touch to complete another more spontaneous creation. Start to combine marks across an area in different ways to build up different styles of shading or texture. Try changing the factors that influence the quality of the mark you make: experiment with different shaped nibs, heat settings, pen angle, time of contact with the wood, pressure, and movement of your hand. All of these variables can help you to create a range of marks you will be able to use as you start to draw. I've completed a range of basic marks and patterns with simple instructions to describe how you can achieve the same effect yourself.

Starting to Draw

In the first three chapters, we looked at making our first decorative lines and marks on wood with the pyrography pen and creating basic areas of shade and tone. We moved on to some figurative designs through the use of silhouettes, which were constructed through blocks of flat shading contained within an outline.

The next stage is to consider drawing with the pyrography pen in a more expressive and flexible manner. This will feature the use of line and tone in different combinations in order to create a visual representation of something. The subject may be realistic or abstract, depending on your preference, but the main focus is to develop your skills for visual representation. This will require you to develop a sensitive eye for changes in tone and a deft touch with the pyrography pen in order to recreate your interpretation.

If you have already studied art in some form or another, you may be familiar with the use of rough sketchbooks to develop ideas and designs. As previously discussed, this method of planning and development is ideal for the pyrographer as the marks a pencil can make are so similar to those made with the pyrography pen. Sketching the world around you with pencil and paper is a good way to develop your artistic ability without using costly pieces of wood for rough experiments all of the time.

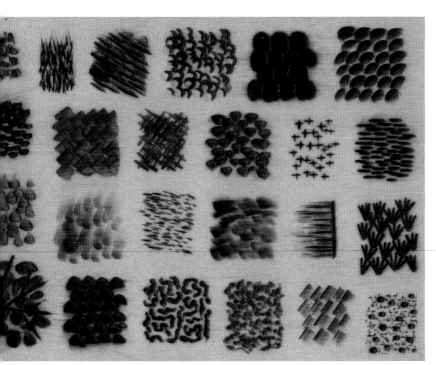

Just because you've singed the wood doesn't mean you can't use the mark. Be open-minded! Many of these marks may be called mistakes or be regarded as imperfect by traditionalists, but who knows what they'll come in handy for?

PRACTICE EXERCISE: QUICK SKETCHING

The aim here is to develop techniques for representing different surfaces, tones, or structures and to build your confidence in applying them as quickly as possible. You'll be creating a scene with your pyrography pen in about ten minutes. Working under pressure in this way can increase your understanding of the capabilities of your pyrography machine. You may be very pleased with the results of what you have achieved in a short period of time, as the marks can be quite spontaneous and unpredictable. When you then move on to creating larger works with more time, you can transfer some of these techniques in order to make your work varied and interesting. This exercise can be carried out with a pencil and paper before you move on to using the pyrography machine.

This exercise will provide you with plenty of experience in constructing and completing larger images. You can practice as many times as you like, and you may find it is an exercise you come back to when you just want to burn to relax rather than to make something specific. If you need subject material, try taking photographs of local landscapes or landmarks so you always have an image to work from, even on a rainy day or at night.

Find a landscape that you like. Study the scene. Consider the difference between solid structures and the softer areas. Look at the shape of areas that are in deep shadow and see how they correspond with well-lit objects. Think about the different marks that you could use to represent these areas.

Now give yourself a short period of time—10 minutes or so—to create an impression of the scene on wood. Sketch or trace the basic details of the scene onto your piece of wood in pencil so that the structure is in place ready for you to burn.

Start to burn from the background toward the foreground, using smaller marks that become bolder as you get closer to the foreground. You may be able to see individual leaves on a tree that is close to you, but you can't make them out on the trees several hundred yards away.

Use any nibs you have available to create a range of marks. Each mark should give the impression of a different texture or surface. Use dots, lines, dashes, spirals, and any other form of mark that feels right to recreate a certain object or area.

Drawing on Shaped and Small Items

As your confidence in drawing with the pyrography pen grows, you will probably want to explore the many ways that you can create decorative images on wooden objects. Because pyrography is not limited to the constraints of working on two-dimensional surfaces such as paper, you will no doubt wish to experiment with the range of wooden objects available. Pyrography blanks are available from numerous suppliers in many shapes and sizes. As you expand your experience from large flat surfaces, there are some considerations to keep in mind.

Curved faces

Many lathe-turned objects are available as burning blanks. These include curved or spherical faces, which can provide a challenge to a pyrographer who is starting out. It is possible to transfer images onto a curved surface using tracing paper, especially if you use masking tape to secure the paper in place while you work. If the curve is more three-dimensional, the paper will not sit easily on the surface, which means you cannot transfer an image onto it without it being extremely distorted. When working on shaped objects, you will need to allow for these limitations in your initial plans. This may mean you have to draw an image entirely freehand or break the design down into smaller segments you can manage to transfer using a basic stencil, template, or tracing paper.

Working on shaped objects can be awkward at times depending on their size and shape. We are used to writing on flat surfaces and rely on the surrounding area to provide steady support for our hand as we work. This may not be possible on some turned items as there may be no natural resting place for your hand as you try to burn. If this is the case, try to make an impromptu rest for your hand using other flat items, such as a book or some coasters. These will allow you to build up an area next to the item you are burning so you can support your hand as fully as possible. The rest you make should give you a working height parallel to the top edge of the wooden item, so the pen nib is at a natural writing angle to burn with.

Adjust the height you work at in any way you find practical. When working on large turned bowls or vases, I have rested them on my knees and held them against the edge of the worktop to prevent movement. This has allowed me to then use the table edge as the rest for my hand. The item can also be readily rotated or adjusted as the design progresses.

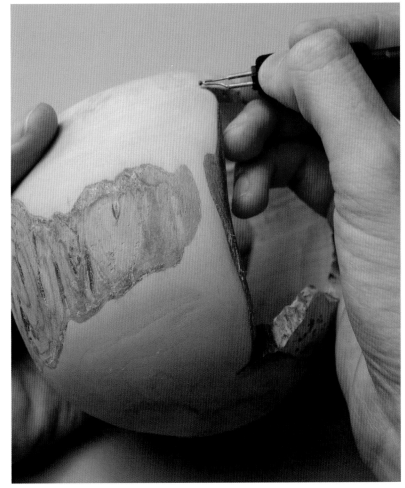

Make sure you have a firm grip on a curved or shaped object when you are working, as a slip may result in a mistake in the design or a burn to your fingers!

Small items

Care needs to be taken when you are working on smaller round items, such as miniature pots or eggs. Your fingers and hand will be a lot closer to the nib as you work if you try to hold them during the burning process. If you work on small items regularly, it may be worth investing in an item such as a vise or clamp that will hold the object securely while you work. Any vise will need to be used carefully so that you do not leave scratches, marks, or indentations in the wooden surface. A shaped wooden table hook is also a useful option, as it allows the object to be held at only one end while you work. You may be able to get one made to your own specification with adjustable pegs to assist in securing items as you work.

Small items in general can be challenging to work on, as even the smallest error will be more likely to be noticed. However, small items can be rewarding as they can be completed quickly, and successful or popular designs can be reproduced with ease. The shape of a small item, such as a key ring fob, may also inspire you to create a design based on that particular form.

Drawing Borders

As you start to use pyrography on more ornate crafted objects, decorative borders will provide stunning artistic results regardless of your skill level. Adding a border involves working in a small and defined area, but the subject potential is vast. The border decoration can be pictorial (such as a landscape or image); patterned (using repeated symbols or images in a structured way); or textural (decorated to represent another surface or appearance). The patterns may be geometric, organic, Celtic, modern, regular, random, or any approach you care to apply. It may include words, letters, or numbers for a range of purposes. A border can be as simple or as complicated as you like.

When you are planning a border, work out the boundaries and mark them onto the surface with pencil as the first stage. Many wooden items lend themselves naturally to a border due to the way they are made: photo frames feature a narrow rectangular area a border can be applied to, while many wooden plates or bowls often have a turned rim defined by a groove or lip. Decide whether your border will go right up to an edge or whether it will be separated by a gap.

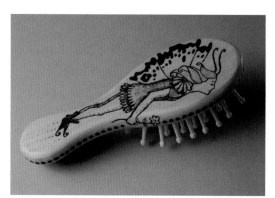

When working on a curved or shaped surface, the image can be positioned to flow around the form.

I decorated this jewelry box with a simple garland pattern to form a border around the glass panel.

Break down any areas into equal segments to help plan a border. The preparation can be constructed lightly in pencil so it is easy to remove once you have burned the design into the wood.

Borders do not have to be symmetrical or have regular repeated symbols. This frame uses a segmented border with random plant images yet still frames the photo contained within.

If your border design has important key features, mark out the required spacing at regular intervals in pencil to ensure that the design is as balanced as possible. The circles marked on this photo frame edge indicate where flower motifs will be added.

Corner motifs are a useful way to cope with a change of direction in a border design. They can also add more visual interest to the design, rather than struggling to make the pattern flow around the frame.

The next step is to start drawing out the content of your border design. If the design is quite loose, organic, or random, drawing it on freehand without planning is probably the most appropriate method to help create a more haphazard appearance in keeping with the subject.

If the border features a carefully structured pattern, you will need to plan the design more rigorously to ensure that it is successful. This may include dividing the available space into equal sections. If the pattern is based on identical and repeated elements, measuring the available space and dividing it into equal segments will help you keep the layout balanced and consistent. You may also want to experiment with borders that are broken into sections or are more irregular in their structure.

Measuring the space in your border will help you to place key visual elements regularly across the space that you are working on. If you are working on a floral or plant design, for example, you may want to measure how often a flower head appears throughout the border. Once these key features have been added, you can then fill the remaining space with secondary decoration, such as smaller leaves, tendrils, or buds.

Consider what happens at any corners your border will include. A corner signifies a change in direction so your pattern will need to be planned to deal with that factor. You may wish to add a motif or separate design element at the corner so the border can alter its course smoothly without the need to alter the flow or rhythm. Some designs lend themselves naturally to moving around a corner or angle, while others may look forced, ungainly, or lose their visual appeal as a result of a change.

Thorough planning and consideration of various design possibilities at the early stages will prevent you from creating a pyrography design that does not work successfully.

Not Feeling Artistic?

Once you start drawing with your pyrography machine on a regular basis, your confidence will grow and hopefully your enjoyment will increase along with it. The possibilities for drawing in pyrography are boundless and there is plenty of scope to find your own methods of expression and personal style. However, if you do not feel confident drawing your own more detailed designs in freehand, there are numerous ways that you can find assistance in creating images for your craft. Many pyrographers rely on stencils or similar items to create their designs, as their enjoyment comes from the creation of the image on the wood rather than the creation of the image itself from scratch.

Design sourcebooks

There are countless design sourcebooks aimed at the craft market that feature ready-to-use images for all purposes. The range of themes available is impressive, including the following topics: Celtic and medieval designs; fairies and angels; dragons and mythological creatures; Chinese; Japanese; Art Deco; Art Nouveau; Christmas; Halloween; flowers and plants; animals and birds; and lots more topics to suit all tastes. These books often include a range of images, borders, patterns, and lettering that will help any crafter to decorate an item in a specific style or appearance. The content can be traced, photocopied, enlarged, reduced, or used in combination to suit your own needs and requirements, so they are a useful source of reference if you decide to use them.

Internet

The Internet is an invaluable resource to help you in your quest to find suitable designs for pyrography as well. Web sites that contain free clip art or other images for general use can easily be adapted for applying to your blank canvas. It is easy to resize such images on your home computer using even the most basic imaging application so you can print the image and trace it for transferring. Many of these sites state that the images contained are published in the public domain for general use. Remember you will have to obtain permission from the owner if you wish to use an image subject to copyright.

Stencils

The boom in Do It Yourself (D.I.Y.) has also provided a useful tool. The recent trend for stencilling as a home decoration technique led to the creation and retail of ready-made stencils, as well as books and guides to assist you in creating your own. A stencil can be the simplest way to mark out an image ready to be burned on your material of choice, yet it does not have to limit your imagination. The other benefit to using a stencil is it makes it so easy to repeat a motif if you are creating a pattern or a number of identical pieces. Obviously, a stencil will only provide you with the most basic of outlines, so it is down to you then to decide how you will complete the image through further tonal work or similar to achieve the finish you desire.

The next chapter in the book focuses on the use of patterns and textures in more detail, and expands on the practical use of them decoratively for features in your designs such as borders. We will cover tips and advice for more detailed drawing in some of the later chapters, when we look at portraits and other figurative work.

DRAWING SYMMETRICAL DESIGNS

If any of the elements in a design you work on are symmetrical, you can save time by tracing or drawing half of the image along the line of reflection. This method is particularly useful if you do not feel confident in drawing lines freehand that need to form symmetrical images: curves can be very difficult to construct with, due to the natural restricted movement in our wrists.

1

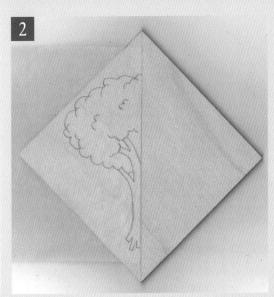

2

Draw half of the image onto a piece of tracing paper. You can use the straight edge of the paper as your line of reflection.

Draw a line on your wooden surface that will act as the line of reflection as well as mapping where the image will be placed. Turn the paper over and place it onto the piece of wood. Draw carefully over the reverse of the tracing to transfer the first half of the image onto the wood.

3

4

Turn the tracing paper back over and carefully line up both parts of the image to form the whole design. Draw carefully over the mirror image of the tracing to transfer the remaining section of the pattern.

Once the symmetrical design has been successfully transferred, you can draw the rest of the design onto the wood ready for the pyrography.

Landscapes are a popular subject for any art or crafts technique. The scope of different landscapes available for inspiration is immense. Your landscape may include modern buildings, ancient castles, trees, deserts, hills, mountains, monuments, ruins, or a million other possibilities. The landscape you choose to recreate may be one that you see every day, one from far away that you have always dreamt of visiting, or one that is entirely fictional from your own imagination.

In this project, we will make a wooden picture postcard with a landscape view. You can frame this or display it in your home to remind you of a place you have visited or a scene you like, or you may want to give it to a friend as a present. The size of the item is large enough to give you room to explore what you can do with your machine, but not so large that it becomes overwhelming or a chore if you are still a beginner.

These principles apply whatever the subject matter, so practice your pyrography drawing skills on a range of landscapes or scenes. Remember to be sensitive to what you can see and how it looks, and you may develop some techniques or textures that are perfect for certain surfaces or materials. You may want to move onto creating larger and more challenging pieces of pyrography art, so enjoy the freedom of expression your new skills will bring.

TOOLS & MATERIALS

- Pyrography machine
- Pencil
- Eraser
- Flat piece of wooden sheet, approximately 8" x 6" (200mm x 150mm)
- Photograph of a landscape to work from

1. Preparation

This photograph of Leeds Castle in Kent was taken by Terry Wren. I selected it due to the textural contrast between the building and surroundings, as well as my fascination with castles!

Decide what sort of wooden item you want to create your landscape on. You may be able to purchase a wooden blank from a craft supplier that is a suitable size, such as a placemat, plaque, or large coaster. Your local D.I.Y. or hardware store may stock a range of suitable timber sheets. You can choose to work on birch plywood or any other wood.

If this is the first time you have worked on a landscape, I would suggest you choose to work from a photograph to start with. The photograph depicts a moment frozen in time, so there will be no changes in lighting or adverse weather conditions to deal with as you work. Look through your photograph albums to find a photo that appeals to you. Try to select one with a range of different structures, textures, and features included so you will have plenty of opportunities to test your pyrographic abilities. Look for an image with a range of tones across the whole scene, from dark shadow to pale highlights.

If you wish, you can always use the photograph I have used in this project and work through each step following my examples for guidance.

2. Map the Structure

Begin by mapping out the basic structure of the image on tracing paper. Try to keep the proportions of the image as accurate as possible. If possible, print the image you have chosen to the required size, as similar as possible to the size of your wooden canvas. You can then simply trace the details and transfer them across exactly.

An alternative way to build up the basis of your image is the grid method, which is particularly useful if your pyrography image will be larger than the source photo itself. Divide the source image into squares, either by drawing on a copy of the photo or placing a transparent tracing paper grid over it. You can then use the grid for reference as you transfer the details across, helping you to position the reference points correctly and as accurately as possible.

I traced the basic structure and details of the scene onto tracing paper.

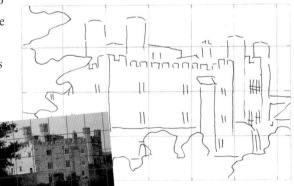

By placing a grid over your original photograph, you can reproduce the image on your larger canvas by using a bigger grid and transferring the image freehand square by square, keeping the proportion.

3. Transfer to the Wood

Draw as much information as you need to help you construct the basic details of the entire landscape. You do not need to make an extremely detailed pencil drawing of the image because you will be burning over it, so just use as many lines as you need to mark out the key points and main areas to work with. If the tracing is a little faint or you feel you need to add more details before you start burning, draw the additional lines in by pencil until you are satisfied you have enough information to work from.

Decide how you are going to tackle the subject. In the photograph on page 93, the main feature is the castle, so it will be the focus of attention in the drawing. On the left hand side, there is some dark foliage in the foreground that moves in front of the castle that is best left until last, so disregard it for now.

4. Begin to Burn

Get your pyrography machine ready and select an appropriate nib. I'm going to start by adding some of the darkest areas, such as the windows and other areas in shadow. Most of these are quite small so choose an appropriate nib for the detail, such as a blade or the edge of a small spoon point nib at a medium to high temperature setting. Using the tip of the nib gives you a lot of control over the area that you will burn, and you can use the long edge of the blade in the same way as a skew to create longer straight lines.

5. Add Texture

After studying the castle in detail, I observed that the roof and chimney stacks appeared to be made of modern bricks and materials compared to the rest of the castle. I decided to use a small chisel nib to create the required textures. The straight tip of these nibs can be pressed in to

create short lines, or used at different angles to create a cross-hatched effect: this is particularly useful when you want to give an impression of bricks. I created long parallel lines with the chisel to represent the slates on the sloping roof areas. I pressed the tip of the chisel in at intervals to create the shadows under the battlements at the top of the castle.

The pencil outline was transferred onto the wood ready for burning to begin.

I started by adding the darkest details and areas of shadow with a fine bladed nib.

I then started adding the brick texture to the roof and chimney sections using the sharp edge of a small chisel nib.

I then added some finer details and shadow lines using a medium skew.

Wall textures were created using the bowl of a spoon point nib or a chisel, depending on the quality of the bricks depicted.

The remaining outlines to define the castle towers and corners were added with the tip of a skew to create fine, broken lines.

6. Add Finer Details

The next stage is to add some of the finer details that build up the structure of the image. Use a medium skew to add sharp lines where required. The lines do not have to be solid and even. You can use broken or uneven lines to represent crumbling or irregular surfaces or edges. Use the tip of the skew to add shade in small areas by dragging it along in small strokes. Adjust the temperature where necessary to change the line quality, reducing the setting to create fine sharp lines.

7. Add Mid-tones

The next stage was to add some of the smaller areas of texture that fall into the mid-tonal range. I used the bowl of a spoon point nib to create a range of textures. I dabbed the bowl repeatedly to create the old stone wall in the bottom left of the picture. I created a smoother consistent tone for the horizon and top roof in the middle by moving the bowl constantly in small circles over the wood. I also used the chisel tip again to add some more modern brickwork.

8. Add Outlines

The next stage was to add any more structural lines that were still required before I moved onto the substantial shading of the castle walls. I used the tip of a skew to add straight lines around the top of each turret, and broken lines along the corner edges where two walls joined.

9. Add Shading

The shading stage was the most time-consuming part of the project because the castle walls formed the majority of the scene. I used the bowl of a spoon point nib to create a slightly dappled surface, in keeping with the rough stonework on show. I started with a low temperature setting for the wall that the light was falling on the most, which slightly burnished the surface with only a minimal color change. I then increased the temperature a little more each time I moved onto a wall that was more shaded. I used three different tones and shaded the castle walls accordingly, creating a sense of solidity and form in the drawn structure. Remember to leave areas free from any burning if you want them to act as highlights in the image.

10. Add Accents

The walls still look a little even and regular at this stage, so the irregular nature of the hewn stone bricks needs to be emphasized. I used the tip of a spear shader to create random bricks across the surface of the darker castle walls, repeatedly pushing the tip in at a slight angle and pulling it down to create a series of tiny irregular rectangles. On the wall that had a lot of light shining on it, I reduced the temperature of the spear shader nib and pressed it gently in at random intervals to create the barest impression of brickwork through short irregular lines.

11. Burn the Midground

Now that the castle was basically complete, it was time to move forward to the wall and climbing vegetation that crosses in front of the building. I added the wall using a chisel nib, creating a solid dark line across the top and then dragging the nib repeatedly in a downward motion at irregular intervals to shade it. I then used a ball stylus nib on a medium temperature setting to start to

I used three different temperature settings to shade the castle walls with the bowl of a spoon point nib. As the setting was increased, a deeper shadow was created.

I used the tip of a spear shader to create random marks across the walls, giving the impression of masonry or stonework.

I started to add some of the vegetation in front of the castle using a ball stylus nib on a medium setting.

I added some more definition by dabbing the tip of a circle shader at different angles to create random shadows.

I used a spear shader on a high temperature to create the dark branches in the foreground, pressing and flicking the nib into the wood to make leaf shapes.

Now the drawing is complete. I constructed a border around the image to frame it.

add the leafy vegetation climbing over the wall, building up a mass of small dots.

To add more substance to the vegetation, I used the nib of a circle shader on a medium/high temperature setting, dabbing the nib around at differing angles to create a soft pattern of arcs and semi-circles to simulate leaves and shadows.

12. Burn the Foreground

It is now time to tackle the tree branches in the foreground closest to the viewer. I utilized one of my favorite textural techniques for this. I used a spear shader on a high temperature, pressing the tip firmly into the surface and dragging or flicking it to create random leaf shapes. Draw a few irregular lines with the point to represent branches, and you create a very successful foliage effect in silhouette. This effect is very bold and vivid, which emphasizes the fact it is closer to the viewer than the castle, which is formed by its softer, subtler marks.

13. Create a Border

The image itself is now finished and you need to decide whether you want to add a border to frame the drawing. I decided a ⅛" (3mm) frame would finish the design well, so I constructed the edges with a pencil and ruler. I drew the lines of the border with a skew and then blocked it in using the flat face of a circle shader. As you have now completed a piece of art, don't forget to add your signature: you never know…it may be worth something one day! Use a fine blade or similar to add your autograph neatly near the bottom edge. You can treat the finished design with Danish oil or leave the wood untreated, depending on your own personal preference.

Chapter 5

Texture and Pattern

The use of texture has always been very important in my work, as it can be used to give objects a personality that defines how they are used and regarded. The tactile quality provided by texture is very important to me: I like making items you cannot resist picking up and turning around in your hands, admiring from all angles and feeling the warmth and sensation of the wooden item with your fingers. By changing the smooth surface of a piece of wood with a pyrography nib, you will start to create a texture dependent on the way you apply the heat. Textures can be found just about everywhere—have a good look around and you'll see many ideas and inspirations just during your daily routine.

Pattern and texture can be one and the same, or they can be completely separate. Patterns are primarily visual rhythms that may be applied in such a way that they do not create a sense of texture. Pyrography patterns often create a texture due to the application of heat to change a surface. Check out the texture and pattern appendix on page 201 for even more ideas.

This pear bowl was decorated with a pattern inspired by close examination of the cross-section of a piece of bone.

About Texture

I have always sought to explore the relationship between pattern, texture, and form, and how each influences the other. My fascination with these elements has led me to consider issues such as:

- The relationship between the inner and outer form of an object.
- The location and amount of texture or pattern used on a form.
- The idea of texture or pattern as a parasite, dictating on and imposing over the form it occupies.
- The use of visual rhythm and repeatable elements in a design.
- How texture and pattern influences and emphasizes details about a piece, i.e., the location of apertures, openings, fittings, and mechanisms.

I like to produce pieces that intrigue the user and create an emotional link with them. I am interested in the idea that we express our personalities by the objects that we surround ourselves with. Many of our possessions are simply functional products we need for day-to-day life, but we also have items that mean something to us personally. There are many different reasons for this psychological connection to a physical product: it may have been a gift from a loved one, something that brings back memories from the past, or be a favorite possession for reasons we cannot fully explain in words. Such objects often have a greater emotional value than their intrinsic financial worth. It is interesting how certain items can leap out at us, whether it is an expensive ring in a shop display or a smooth pebble on a beach. It is not possible to create products that appeal to everyone in the same way, but it can be a useful consideration when designing an item for a special occasion. The main inspiration for me has always been my

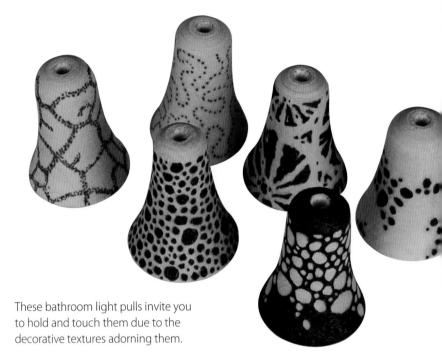

These bathroom light pulls invite you to hold and touch them due to the decorative textures adorning them.

immediate surroundings. I find myself constantly looking at things and trying to discover something about them, the way they are, and how they work. Photography has been a personal hobby for many years, and I have found it increasingly useful in my study to show how I interpret both objects I find and my own work.

Finding Textures and Patterns

Patterns can be found around you wherever you look. Common patterns include stripes, dots, zigzags, squares, and rectangles. A good place to start would be items that have had a pattern applied to them deliberately: this may include items of clothing, fabric, wallpaper, prints, or other items with a decorative purpose. Our opinions and ideas about patterns are often formed through our appreciation of such designs, which are usually based on images or motifs regularly repeated on a two-dimensional flat surface.

Patterns are not limited to the work of graphic or textile designers, and they certainly do not have to be restricted and measured by regularity. Some of the most interesting and thought-provoking patterns can be irregular, unpredictable, and often entirely accidental, making the inspiration they provide for a designer even more valuable and unique.

Patterns can be found in everything that surrounds you, 24 hours a day, 7 days a week. Start by considering the room in which you are working or the house in which you live. Consider the way you have arranged or positioned the items around you: the pattern of books arranged on a shelf, or pictures on a wall. Look at the way you stack tins of food in a cupboard, or utensils in a drawer. The relationship between these items, and the shapes and spaces created when they interact, all form natural patterns that may never occur again.

Look at the materials that items in your house are made from: do they contain natural patterns? We use one of the most richly decorative materials regularly during our pyrography sessions: each species and type of wood is unique with different patterns formed by the figure and grain. Start to consider the pattern inherent in other items around you. For example, consider the pattern of a piece of knitted garment, the metal mesh of a kitchen utensil, or the layout of buttons and dials on electric goods. Each of these studies may result in a spark of inspiration that becomes the basis for a decorative pattern or texture.

Once you've been bitten by the pattern-seeking bug, you may find entirely new avenues to seek out sources for creative reflection. The commute to work, usually a routine that becomes a chore, may provide numerous possibilities once you open your eyes to what surrounds you: windows on the side of a building, the hubcap on a passing car, a line of people with umbrellas in the rain. A fleeting glimpse that lasts no longer than a second may leave a visual impression on your mind: you may wish to get yourself a small sketchbook to keep close at hand for recording these moments. It would gradually build up over time into a design sourcebook, full of useful sketches, notes or cut-out images that may be just what you are looking for one day when you've hit a creative brick wall!

Bricks make a fascinating pattern. Often it is assumed that bricks are geometric and identical, but actually they're full of character and wear.

Flowers display so much variety and beauty, and form extremely complex natural patterns when viewed together.

Some patterns found around the home are completely unpredictable, such as the effects of evening sunlight through frosted glass and a blind.

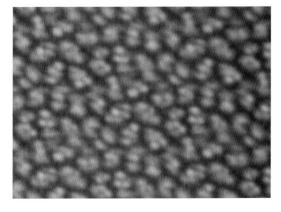

Stencils

As already mentioned, stencils are frequently used by crafters to assist with the creation of decorative designs in their work. When you are working at creating designs with identical elements, stencils provide greater accuracy and allow you to work more quickly than working freehand. You don't have to purchase readymade stencils to use the technique of stenciling: consider which patterns or textures you have discovered that can be used to physically construct and create your own design.

If you wish to create a pattern design, the easiest place to start is with items that are already on hand in your own home. Many objects have interesting shapes that can form decorative patterns when repeated, such as keys or coins. If you have young children in your home, a rummage through their toy boxes may reveal blocks, bricks, or other shapes you can either draw around or through. I found a plastic tray in my daughter's toys with a hexagonal mesh design—I was able to draw through it to create a honeycomb pattern in no time at all.

You can often scan items into your computer so that you can create your own design layouts with minimal effort. I found this ivy leaf while out walking, and decided to keep a digital copy for future reference.

I used the ivy leaf scan, along with other similar images, as the inspiration for this wooden bangle design. Each leaf shape was different to the previous one on the bracelet, making the design unique from every angle.

The hexagonal pattern on this box was created using a child's toy. It was perfect for creating a honeycomb pattern easily and quickly.

MAKING A STENCIL

If you cannot find an item to suit your needs, you can always create your own impromptu stencils from stiff card stock or a sheet of thin plastic. Mark out the required shape lightly with a sharp pencil, making sure that it is accurate and correctly proportioned. Before you start to cut, place the card or plastic onto a protective surface, such as a cutting mat or piece of scrap wood. Carefully cut the shape out using a craft scalpel. Take your time to make sure that you do not slip and cut your fingers. It is better to make several light cuts than to press too hard trying to go through the material in one go. Once completed, you have a stencil that you can use to mark out the same shape as often as you want. You can keep all of your homemade stencils in a folder or box for future use as well, so that you build up an extensive source of working materials.

Once you become interested in the possibilities of patterns created naturally by the items around you, it may be useful to collect objects that interest you to form a library of inspiration. You can store interesting items such as pebbles, leaves, or bottle caps. You can also scan items and store them digitally, which is particularly useful for natural materials that may deteriorate over time.

Geometry

Geometric designs often look simple but can actually be complex. Because they are often based on repeated basic shapes, they can be simple to plan and construct using stencils, rulers, or compasses. You can always produce your own template from card or plastic as described in the sidebar (left).

When working on geometric designs, you will need to have a steady hand. It is easier to make a mistake on designs such as these, as one misplaced line can throw the whole pattern out of sync. Taking time to plan the design on the surface is vital to prevent mistakes during the burning stage. Geometric designs often rely strongly on smooth curved or straight lines, so skews and blades are particularly useful when you need to ensure the quality of the lines involved.

Geometric designs can be extremely difficult to master but are definitely worth the effort.

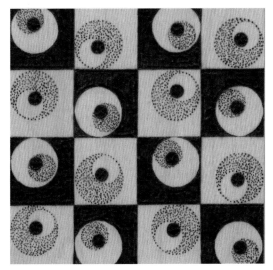

Complex and Exotic Patterns

Many patterns from around the world have now become an everyday part of our lives. One good example of this is the popularity of animal prints in designs today. Patterns based on the markings of the leopard, tiger, zebra, cow, and many more are used in designs for textiles and other household items. The patterns can all be adapted for use with pyrography if you wish: perhaps as a one-off decorative item or a range of wildlife-themed designs.

I have always loved the natural pattern found on leopard fur.

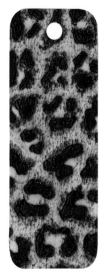

Animal patterns are particularly versatile. They can be simplified as a pattern so they are constructed in just two tones if required, like a silhouette. On the other hand, you can make them as realistic as possible by trying to create the impression of fur in a range of tones: this will make the whole piece feel more textural. I created

This key ring design was decorated with a leopard print pattern. I used small strokes of the nib over and over again to emulate the appearance of fur.

several patterned boxes using a very simple adaptation of a leopardprint design. The finished works looked like they would be soft to the touch. You may be able to list other examples of sources for such patterns, including plants, rocks, native artwork or decoration, and many more.

Recreating Surface Textures

It is also possible to give your wooden item the appearance of other surfaces through sensitive use of pyrography. Make sure you carry out as much research as you can when attempting this. You can collect pictures or other visual material for reference from a range of sources so you have plenty of reference points from which to work. You may also wish to spend time sketching the surfaces to get a feel for the way you can reproduce them with a pen or pencil. Once you feel prepared, you can then move onto a piece of scrap wood and transfer your experiments to the pyrography machine. In this way, you may be able to recreate the appearance of a range of surfaces, including stone, water, sand, fabric, metal, and even wood! That may sound slightly odd, but I have sometimes needed to create the appearance of a wooden texture when working on a piece of wood.

Zooming In

Due to the surroundings of the Wiltshire countryside where I grew up, I have always been interested in natural forms and their individual textures, such as bones, rocks, and plants. This led me to taking close-up shots of surfaces and objects with my camera in order to fully appreciate the texture, pattern, and structure of them. Experimenting with macro lenses and other photographic equipment can provide some very rewarding results.

Once the use of my camera had got me as close as possible with the equipment I was using, I began to look elsewhere for ways to move in even closer. I became increasingly interested in microscopes and the intriguing images that can be seen when using them. Items that have been studied for scientific purposes can reveal a stunning natural beauty or elegance that is not usually apparent to the naked eye. Studying old

Macro photography can be used to create close-up studies of items and surfaces, such as this lily.

I took this photograph of an old tree trunk several years ago, and recently used the photograph as the basis for a pattern in pyrography based on the bark formation.

The design on the rim of this plate was based on a study drawn from a photograph of molten metal over a glass surface.

scientific textbooks for inspiration was an unusual but fruitful avenue to explore.

Suddenly you will realize you are actually limited by the use of your eyes alone and will need to find new techniques to continue your quest for patterns and textures. Why not use a pattern based on your own fingerprint or the wings of a butterfly? Inspiration may be found through the lens of a microscope or magnifying glass, when you are suddenly able to appreciate an item with a completely fresh outlook on the beauty that had been hidden from you. Don't be afraid to use whatever technology you have at your disposal—photocopiers, scanners, photo manipulation software on your computer—you never know what sort of patterns you'll find.

This frame was decorated with a bold pattern that is a personal favorite of mine, based on the natural patterns found in coral.

This pattern was based on studies of ripples made on the beach by the retreating waves of the sea.

PRACTICE EXERCISE: CREATING ZOOMED-IN DESIGNS

There are many technological processes that can help you with your search for patterns. When looking to decorate a wooden bowl with a fingerprint design, I created my own fingerprint on paper using black ink and a roller...basically the same way that fingerprints would have been taken in the past at a police station! I then took the fingerprint and photocopied it, setting the machine to enlarge the fingerprint at the maximum setting of 200%. I repeated this a few more times, each time placing the largest image back into the copier and enlarging it again. Eventually I had a fingerprint that was about the size of a small dinner plate. I copied it using tracing paper and transferred it onto the wooden bowl.

Make a fingerprint with black ink and paper.

The pattern of the fingerprint made an interesting decorative motif that would not have been easy to recreate by drawing freehand. You could easily apply this technique to many other ideas or images, which would help you to create an individual result each time.

Photocopy the fingerprint by 200%. Continue to enlarge the enlargements until you find a pattern you're pleased with.

Key ring fobs are a good item to use for exploring new patterns or textures. As they only have a small surface area, they can be completed quickly yet still allow you to explore new ideas and patterns. The added advantage they have over experimenting on scrap pieces of wood is they form a useful item and have a purpose once completed. You can also scan or photograph them very easily to keep a visual record of patterns and textures you may wish to incorporate into a larger design at a later date. This effect can be applied to literally any visual design or motif you wish to use in your work.

As well as small items, you could use a textural effect to decorate a larger piece, such as the edge of a photo frame or plate. The potential scope for textural inspiration is vast and you will find ideas wherever you look around you.

1. Choose a Texture

For my project, I have decided to recreate the textural appearance of an old stone surface. The idea came to me after looking at old carved stonework such as gravestones and the like at a local churchyard. Due to the sense of history and age I intend to give the surface, I selected an ancient symbol to include as the carved feature of the design. "Awen" is the Welsh word for "inspiration" and it is often represented by the Druids through an emblem of circular rings featuring three lines radiating from three circles or dots.

The Awen symbol is simple and fits with the texture I've selected.

2. Draw the Design

The first stage is to draw the design lightly onto the chosen fob with a pencil. I chose a circular wooden fob so the emblem could fill the whole surface. I started by drawing the three circular rings around the outside of the fob. I used the tip of my finger as a guide to draw the rings, rather than using a pair of compasses: I was not worried that the lines had to be exact or accurate in any way as the rough nature of them adds to the sense of history. After the rings, I drew the triangular shapes and small circles to form the rest of the Awen symbol.

3. Burn the Outline

I then fixed a spoon point nib into my pyrography machine and turned it on at a high temperature. I used the fine edge of the nib to mark out each of the three concentric rings around the fob. I worked fairly quickly and deliberately to make sure the lines were uneven and broken in places. This gave the lines a coarse appearance in keeping with the crumbling effect I wanted to create.

The next stage was to complete the outline of the emblem's central features. I used a medium setting on the pyrography machine and drew these lines very lightly with the edge of the nib so that they were finer in appearance. I still allowed the lines to be broken in places as with the outer rings.

4. Shade the Darkest Tones

Once the lines are completed, the next step to start is the shading process. I set the machine to a medium-high setting and held the pen so I was able to use the soft bowl of the spoon point nib. I then added some soft shading around the outermost ring on the fob, dabbing the pen and moving it in a random way along the burned line to create a haphazard shadow. I then shaded the dots and lines by imagining the shadows that would be cast by a light source if the features were engraved or carved deeper into a flat surface. The effect does not have to be precise: the main aim is to create an impression of a roughly carved surface, so do not labor over the placement of the shading.

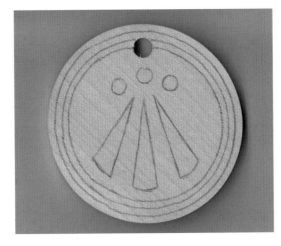

Draw the symbol onto the fob inside three concentric rings.

Use finer broken lines to draw the Awen symbol.

Use the bowl of a small spoon point nib to start adding the darkest shadow areas.

5. Shade the Mid-Tones

Once the darkest tones were completed, I turned the pen down to a medium setting and allowed it to cool slightly for a minute or two. I then filled in the central features with a mid-tone, moving the pen in a stippling motion lightly across the surface until I had achieved the required shade. Dotting and dabbing the pen in this way gives the surface a soft dappled effect, which helps to give the impression that it is rough and pitted. I then added the mid-tone to the outer rings, completely shading the exterior ring and adding some slight shading to the outside of the other two.

6. Add Detail

I then started to add more detail to the image. This helps to create the visual appearance of the surface you are recreating so it is very important to do this carefully. After allowing the pen to cool completely, I turned it on to a very low setting and added some faint highlight lines around the edges of the central features. In addition to helping to define them, this also helps to mark out areas you will leave completely free from burning so they emphasize the form of the carvings. Because the surface is supposed to look like very old stonework, I then turned the pen up to a high temperature and drew random cracks across the surface with the edge of the nib. I held the pen firmly onto the surface at first to make the crack very heavy but then gradually eased the pressure to make the lines fade off to a delicate point.

Add a slightly lighter mid-tone in the next shadow areas, creating a mottled effect by dabbing the pen in a random motion over the surface.

Add some dark cracks at various points with the pen on a high setting.

Use the bowl of the spoon point on a low setting to start adding a base tone around the details added so far.

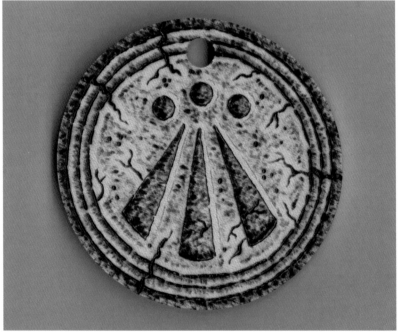

Add some dark dots and stippled marks to make the surface seem more pitted and uneven.

7. Complete the Background

The only area left to complete at this stage is the area around the central features. After allowing the pen to cool again, I set the pyrography machine to a low-medium setting and started coloring the surface using small circular motions with the bowl of the nib. I stayed away from any of the cracks to highlight them with the unburned wood, as well as avoiding going over the highlight lines I had drawn faintly. The general aim is to create a base tone to build on: if you start too dark too soon, you may affect the appearance of the central features by reducing the contrast that should make them stand out.

The final touch was to add a little more shading over the base tone from the last step to finish off the rough texture of the surface. I turned the pen up slightly to a medium setting and used the bowl again to darken random areas across the surface. I even added a few random dots with the point of the nib to increase the bumpy feel of the design.

Once the key ring was finished, I treated the fob with Danish oil to give the wood a warm luster. After adding the metal ring, the design is complete and ready to use.

Chapter 6

Lettering

One of the most enjoyable elements of any handicraft is the ability to create unique gifts that can be personalized with a name, message, or other special feature. Personalized items have more meaning to the recipient, especially when it is clear a design has been created specifically for them alone. Being able to add someone's name to a special gift can feel like the icing on the cake, especially if they have an unusual name that can't usually be found on personalized gifts in the shops.

Incorporating lettering in your pyrography designs can be a demanding skill, requiring a lot of practice and effort, but the finished effect is definitely worthwhile. It is so easy in this day and age to type up text on a computer—the art of beautiful handwriting almost seems to be dying out. Developing your skills in pyrography to create stylish and decorative lettering to a high standard will add another string to your creative bow, and there are a range of techniques available that can assist you as you learn.

This sign was made on a piece of wood with a natural bark edge. I adapted a Celtic font to make the lettering seem more whimsical in line with the dreamlike qualities of the fantasy landscape.

Handwriting as a Starting Point

As with many of the previous exercises, the best place to start is with your pyrography machine and a piece of scrap wood to experiment on. To get the hang of producing letters and words, it makes sense to begin with your own style of handwriting. Use a standard wire looped nib, which is often referred to as a writing nib or writer. The rounded tip makes it ideal for the frequent changes in direction across the surface, as it is similar to the end of a ballpoint pen. Start with a low to medium heat and try various letters of the alphabet before moving onto complete words. Adjust the temperature setting from time to time to see how that affects the results.

If you have purchased any specialist nibs for your pyrography machine, experiment with these also. Some shapes are more suitable than others for the delicate process of forming letters, and all have their own individual benefits and drawbacks. Bladed nibs can be used to create very crisp lines perfect for neat lettering, but they are not easy to use when trying to create tight curves or sudden changes of direction. You may be able to use larger shading points to create a loose or spontaneous form of lettering that does not require sharp edges or neat lines. As with most creative crafts, there is no definitive right or wrong: let your imagination lead you and you may be pleasantly surprised with the finished result!

As you practice, you will begin to develop a feel for what a particular nib can achieve while writing, or what temperature is best used for a certain technique. You may develop your own unique alphabet based on your own handwriting that you will be able to use in a range of pyrography designs. I often handwrite my website address on the bottom of my creations using my own handwriting for a personal touch. It is also the quickest and most natural way to write because a pyrography pen feels no different than a marker over time.

You can use shading nibs to create loose or chaotic lettering styles of your own design.

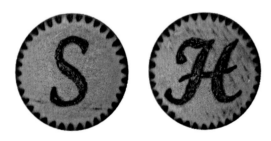

Bladed nibs can be used for very intricate lettering work. These burned initials were added to wooden buttons less than ¾" (20mm) in diameter using a small spear nib.

The edge of a spoon point nib can be used to create the outlines of narrow letters and shade them as well. Burning from end to start will also prevent you from inadvertently rubbing the pencil lettering away as you work with the pyrography machine.

PRACTICE EXERCISE: HANDWRITING

One of the best ways to get into burning letters on wood is to practice on scrap wood with your own handwriting. It should come very naturally to you, whether you're using a pencil or a pyrography machine. I suggest using a writing nib to start, and then expanding your practice to any other specialist nibs you may have on hand.

Practice using your own handwriting on scraps of wood with a pencil. You can try writing in different ways for variety as well.

Burn over the handwriting as neatly as possible, using a blade or writing nib. You can try this a number of times until you are happy with the results.

Choosing the Appropriate Style

I developed the lettering for the name "Freya" on this trinket box from a single letter R that I had seen in a book. I wanted the text to have an elegant decorative feel.

The lettering on this key ring design was selected because it was bold, striking, and crisp, which meant it would work well in a small design.

Countless alphabets and fonts are available around the world. When you start to plan the addition of lettering in your pyrography designs, you will need to consider what effect you wish to create to benefit and enhance the feel of your item. The font or style of lettering you choose needs to be suitable for the intended purpose. It wouldn't be ideal to spend hours creating a beautiful and sensitive illustration in pyrography if you then add lettering that is too bold and looks out of place.

Consider what the design you are creating is going to portray or depict. Is it a humorous design to make people laugh? Then perhaps you can select or develop a suitably funny or eccentric alphabet. Likewise, an elegant style of lettering with delicate flourishes may be best suited for a beautiful decorative piece of work. If you are designing an item you want to look antique, you will need to select an appropriate style of lettering to enhance this rather than ruin the hard work you have spent creating a suitable image or feel. A bold and striking font may be the most appropriate style to accompany a strong silhouette design.

This humorous lettering was added to a box for a young boy who loved dinosaurs. I constructed each letter with small hand-drawn bone shapes.

There are countless fonts and lettering styles for you to consider in books and magazines. You can always cut out examples you like and keep them in a file for reference.

Spend time researching suitable lettering styles or planning the layout and form if you are developing your own style of alphabet. Over time, you may be able to build up a research folder of sample letters and alphabets to refer to, consisting of computer printouts, newspaper or magazine clippings, or other visual sources.

Sources for Lettering

As previously discussed, there are many sources available for inspiration when you wish to find a suitable lettering style for your design work. You can find lettering examples in books, magazines, advertisements, and on the Internet. There are also options available to assist you if you do not feel comfortable or confident in creating your own letters from scratch. Most craft, art, and stationery stores stock stencils of several different alphabets: the benefit of these is they can be used repeatedly to create identical lettering with a minimum of effort. Using a stencil can be restrictive as the size of the lettering is fixed but they can be a good starting point for a beginner due to the neat

results you can produce using them. They can be very useful if you find a specific stencil in a font you enjoy using.

There are also design source books available for crafters that provide examples of both individual letters and whole alphabets. These letters can easily be traced as they are for transfer to a wooden surface, or adapted to suit your own needs if you feel particularly creative.

Computer fonts

Computers are an invaluable resource when it comes to lettering designs. Have a look at the number of fonts available in just your regular word processing application: the version I use contains in excess of 175 different font samples. The other advantage of using computer fonts for inspiration is the ease in which you can adjust the size and proportions of the typed words, which is ideal when you want to fit the words onto a particular item for burning.

When I want to create some text for addition to a pyrography design, I follow these simple steps:

1. Measure the height and width of the area where the lettering needs to go on your wooden item. Remember to leave sufficient room above, below, and at each end of the text so the words don't appear cramped.
2. Browse the available fonts to find one suitable and appropriate for the feel of the design you are working on.
3. Type out the section of text you want to add to your design in either a word-processing or image manipulation program. Consider whether you are using just capital letters or a mixture of upper and lower case.

This sign was created using a font that I enlarged on my computer to get the right size before printing it to trace.

PRACTICE EXERCISE: TRANSFERRING BY PIN

If you don't like using tracing paper or find it too messy, there is another technique I have often used for transferring designs onto wood. Prepare a printout or drawing and tack it into position on the wooden item with masking tape, making sure it will not move at all. I then use a sharp pin or needle, pushing it into the outline of the letters at regular intervals so a small impression is made in the wood. The point of a pair of compasses works just as well if the pin point is very fine. Once you have marked out every letter in this way, you can then lightly connect the dots with a sharp pencil to draw the letters to be burned. This method works best for simple and bold fonts: anything too decorative will leave you with a mess of dots to make something from. It is also best suited to wooden surfaces that are very pale in color as well as soft.

Use a sharp point, such as a pin or the point of a pair of compasses, to lightly mark the outline of the lettering by gently pressing through the paper into the wood.

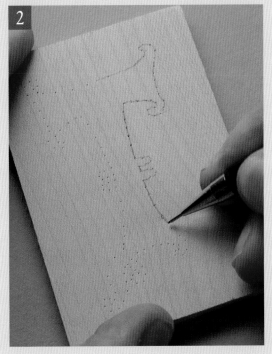

You can then connect the dots lightly with a pencil.

Calligraphy

The art of calligraphy dates back to the days before the printing press and computers, when the handwritten word needed to be clear and legible but was also decorative in its own right. There are many different styles of calligraphic lettering. As a result, there are many books available on the subject.

The calligraphy pen is shaped like a chisel in order to create the combination of bold broader strokes and delicate flourishes or curls. The characteristic appearance of calligraphy is created by the broad nib being applied to the surface at a specific angle. Most alphabets involve the pen being held so that the nib is positioned at a 30–45 degree angle on the paper. When the pen moves horizontally or vertically over the surface, it creates a broad stroke. When it moves up the page in the direction of the angle that the pen is held at, a fine line is created as the broad chisel point moves in the same direction. I would recommend you consider buying a cheap felt-tipped calligraphy pen to practice your technique. It will be cheaper and quicker than practicing your first efforts on pieces of wood with your pyrography machine. Once you get the hang of creating thick and thin strokes using a calligraphy pen, you will understand the basic principle for the way letters are constructed.

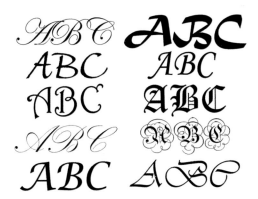

There are many different calligraphic fonts and styles that you can use in your designs, from traditional Gothic to flowing italics.

Calligraphy nibs

There are a number of ways to recreate calligraphic lettering in pyrography designs. Some of the specialist pyrography nibs available are identical to the chisel-shaped tip of a calligraphy pen, so they can be used in exactly the same way to create the bold letters. They can take time to master when you are trying to create neat and clear lettering, as the transfer of heat to mark the wood takes more time to complete than the flow of ink to stain a page. Making a broader stroke can require a slow movement of the pen as the heat spreads from the nib over a larger surface area, making the pen work harder to create the required result. By the same consideration, changing the pen's direction to create a fine line then results in the same amount of heat becoming focused over a smaller area: it is very easy to burn the fine line too heavily and leave a scorched blob if you are not cautious.

You can use a chisel nib to emulate the way a calligraphy pen works...but it does take practice as the point can snag in the wooden surface and lead to uneven burning.

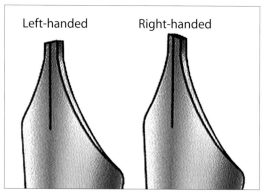

Left-handed   Right-handed

Most standard calligraphy nibs are designed for right-handed use. Left-handed versions are available, and the nib itself is cut at an oblique angle to allow for the different writing position.

If you do decide to purchase a shaped pyrography nib for calligraphy purposes, you will need to bear in mind that the flat chisel-shaped nib can only be used by right-handed people to create lettering in this way. Specialist angled nibs are available for left-handed people to compensate for the slight difference in their natural writing position. It also is possible to shape a pyrography nib in an identical way to form a left-handed calligraphy tip using a jeweler's file if you so wish.

You may not wish to purchase specialist nibs if you are starting out in the early stages of your crafting career, as you may find that the technique is not suited to you or vice versa. Using chisel nibs to form and burn calligraphic lettering can be a very intense process as the nib may snag on the surface, leading to uneven strokes: if you do not feel confident after several practice attempts, then there are other techniques you can use to add calligraphy to your designs.

Freehand calligraphy

Another option is to draw the calligraphy letters freehand and burn them with a more commonly used pyrography nib, as I have done on many occasions with as much success (see Practice Exercise at right). If you are using a calligraphy instruction book to help you with constructing your letters, you will see most alphabets are pictured within parallel tramlines to keep them in proportion. As discussed earlier, proportion is important when constructing letters so you should aim to keep your letters in proportion with those you use for inspiration. Many calligraphy alphabets come with advice on how many nib heights the lower and upper case letters should be to help ensure the letters bear the same proportion to each other no matter what size nib you use. Draw out guidelines to match the nib heights given and you will ensure your letters are constructed as well as possible.

When you have drawn the lettering onto the wood, you are now ready to make it permanent with your pyrography machine. The technique is very similar to that of creating silhouettes, except lettering can be a lot smaller in scale. Use an appropriate fine nib to create the outline of each letter, using a medium heat to avoid unnecessary scorching. It is always better to go over an area a couple of times to get the required results rather than rushing things, which usually results in over-burned marks and a lot of frustration.

Once all of the letter outlines are complete, you can then go on to filling in the broader strokes of the letters with an appropriate shading point. Make sure you do not choose one that is too big for the scale you are working at as you may obliterate some of the fine detail you have created. As I have stated before, a spoon point nib can be ideal for completing lettering: the edge can be used for the outline and then the bowl can be used to complete the shading without stopping to change nibs.

PRACTICE EXERCISE: DRAWING CALLIGRAPHY FREEHAND

I found an easy way to draw calligraphic letters freehand onto wooden surfaces, using two pencils. Make sure both are sharpened well, and then tape them firmly together with sticky tape. If you are right-handed, check that each point touches a flat surface at the same time when the pens are held vertically at right angles to the table. If you are left-handed, the pencils will need to be staggered slightly so they mimic the angle of left-handed calligraphy pens.

This pair of pencils will now form a calligraphy nib, with each point marking the edge of the chisel. Practice using them on rough paper, holding and using them in the same way you would use a calligraphy pen. You should see two parallel pencil lines when the broader strokes would be, and the lines should be closer together (or on top of each other) when the strokes become narrower.

Tape two pencils firmly together to make your impromptu calligraphy pencil. The pencils should be at an angle of between 30-45° when applied to the paper.

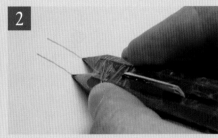

Pulling the pencils directly toward you gives the broadest stroke.

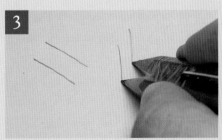

Moving the pencils downward makes a vertical stroke slightly narrower than the previous.

Moving the pencils up and to the right (if you are right-handed) creates the narrow fine lines and flourishes.

Once you have practiced, you can then use the pencils to start drawing your own calligraphy letters to burn.

Pictorial Lettering

There are many beautiful examples of decorative lettering where the letters also incorporate images or pictures, especially on old manuscripts. These are often referred to as "illuminated lettering" because they usually incorporate rich colors and silver or gold leaf to make them more vibrant and ornate. Because they are so decorative and often complicated, they are generally used as the first letter in a title or block of text.

There is no definitive way to create an illuminated letter: just be as artistic as your imagination will allow! Feel free to carry out research to inspire you. You may find you develop design ideas in a sketchbook at first, which gradually evolve into a more defined image over time. If you want to emulate the illuminated lettering in some of the ancient hand-written books, experiment with making large letters with compartments inside that are filled with knotwork or some other element. Another idea for pictorial lettering is to form an image around the letters—this can be difficult, but ultimately rewarding. Another method for changing the lettering would be to make it pictorial, so that each letter is formed by an object or group of items. A curling snake can make a perfect *S* or *C* shape, or a giraffe could be positioned to form the shape of a lower case *h*. A pair of scissors may be used to give the letter *X* and a pair of compasses for the letter *V* if you were working on a design for an artistic person.

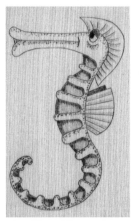

Look around you for shapes and forms that are similar to the letters of the alphabet to help you construct cartoon lettering. This seahorse image was used in one of my designs as the letter J.

The illuminated Chi Rho monogram from the *Book of Kells* is decorated with elaborate knotwork and illustration.

This Latin bible from 1407 AD features an illuminated letter P, starting off the word "Petrus," or Peter in Latin.

This box lid combined the name of the cat with a small portrait, making a perfect personalized gift.

PRACTICE EXERCISE: PLANNING AN ILLUMINATED LETTER

For a basic simple design to start you off, I would suggest you start by drawing out a box with a border in the required position on your wooden item. Use a simple pattern to fill in the border, such as an arrangement of squares or circles. You can then draw a large single letter inside, using any font or style you feel is appropriate.

Decide what sort of image you want to use to decorate the letter. Perhaps you want the letter to be entwined by vines or flowers, twisting back and forth around the form? You could also use animals or any other image that fits in with the design you are working on. The shape of the letter itself may inspire you, such as turning a capital *S* into a hissing snake. The letter may actually form part of a scene or image that is going on around it. Draw and re-draw the design in pencil until you are happy with the letter.

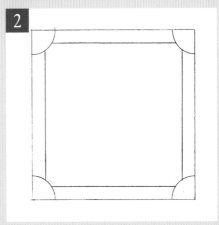

1

Start by drawing a box at the required dimensions for your design.

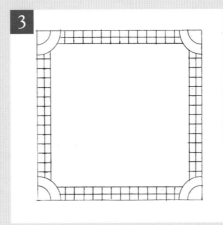

2

Add the basic structure of the decorative or shaped border.

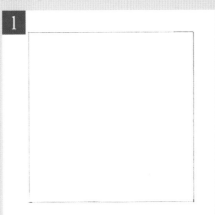

3

Add more detail or pattern to the border in any way that you choose.

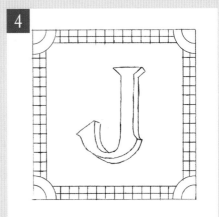

4

Add the capital letter in a font of your choice. Making the letter look three-dimensional is an option.

5

Draw the decorative design or image around the letter. Make the images flow around, over and under the letter to add interest to the design.

PRACTICE EXERCISE: BURNING AN ILLUMINATED LETTER

Once you are satisfied with the drawing, use a blade, writing nib, or similar to carefully draw the outline of the design. Make the letter stand out by shading the inner square background with a very dark tone: this may also give the wood the appearance of a dark, sumptuous leather surface if you take time over it by pressing the bowl of a spoon point nib down in a repeated dabbing motion.

Finish off by adding subtle mid-tone shading or textures where necessary and you will be left with a very striking decorative letter. The options and potential for such designs is infinite and you may find you apply these letters to a range of designs and items. You may go on to develop entire alphabets of decorative pictorial letters. If this style of design is an area you would like to explore further, you may want to consider use of color as an additional feature.

After drawing the planned design onto the wood, draw the outlines with an appropriate nib. I used a skew for the straight lines and the edge of a spoon point for the uneven branches.

Carefully block in the background with a dark tone, using a shading nib. This will increase the visual impact of the design.

Add shading to the main image. I used a shading nib for the letter J and the leaves, but used the point of a skew to add texture to the branches.

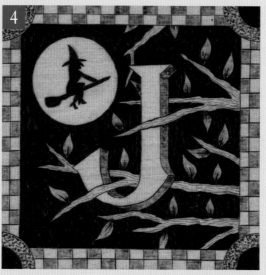

Finish the illuminated letter design by adding shading or textures to the border pattern.

Ambigrams

Ambigrams are a fascinating area of lettering design. The lettering is carefully constructed so it is basically a mirror image of itself: the word is spelled out in the traditional way but also can be read from another angle or direction. There are lots of stunning examples of these intriguing designs available on the Internet if you wish to find out more, and you can then try to create your own. Their popularity is rising due to their inclusion in the book *Angels and Demons* by Dan Brown and the subsequent film, which featured some superb examples of complex amibgrams.

You can use any style of font as the basis to start creating an ambigram. The more decorative the lettering, the easier you may find it to use, as the elegant flourishes can be adapted to show something different when viewed from another angle. Generally, you only need to work on drawing half of the required design: the other half should be created when you turn the first part over!

I spent several hours once designing an ambigram of my wife's name, Jane. I used a traditional Gothic style of calligraphy to write her name and then started to adjust the *J* so that it could also be read as an *E* when inverted. I then followed the same process by making small adjustments to the *A* so that it became an *N* when inverted. I used a small flourish to underline the *N*, but this suddenly became the top stroke of the *A* when turned upside down. It took numerous attempts to create a satisfactory design, but I had great fun trying and the result was worth it.

This key ring features an ambigram of my wife's name. Look at the image upside down…

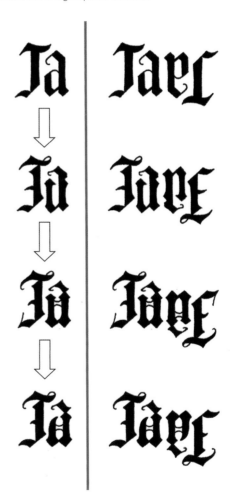

It can take some time to develop an ambigram you are happy with. A letter may work well from one direction, but not be successful when you turn it upside down for its rotated image. Keep adjusting and altering the lettering until you are happy that you have completed a successful design which reads well.

Image courtesy of Greg Williams.

This rotational ambigram reads "vegas" no matter which side is up. Flip the book over and see!

Alternative Alphabets

Once you start building up your confidence in lettering, there are many similar avenues you can explore. There are many other alphabets in different languages that are very intriguing to the eye, such as Chinese, Arabic, or Russian, to name a few. You may wish to carry out research into more historic forms of lettering to add variety to your work. For example, Egyptian hieroglyphics or Norse runes may enhance a design you are working on. You may even be able to use or invent a form of symbolic code to create a design to intrigue the recipient as they try to decipher the message. The options available are limitless, so feel free to experiment with anything that suits you and your crafting.

This personalized picture frame was decorated with Elven text.

Purposes

Once you have used lettering in your pyrography designs on a few occasions, your confidence and abilities will improve steadily. Lettering can be used for a range of purposes as previously mentioned, but ultimately it will provide you with another string to your crafting bow to enrich the designs you create. Adding names and short messages to gifts makes a nice personal touch. Not to mention that adding words can make your work more meaningful—just imagine incorporating song lyrics, sayings, phrases, or poems. You can combine lettering and other skills from this book to create gifts with true meaning to the recipient, due to the feelings or memories they invoke or celebrate.

Adding a couple's names to a photo frame makes a thoughtful romantic gift.

Door signs are very popular items for pyrography. They are important, as they mark out the entrance to a house, room, or other area, giving information to the viewer about where they are or who they may meet. When the sign has been handmade and decorated in a personal style, it may also give the viewer an insight into the character or personality of the people within.

TOOLS & MATERIALS

- Wooden plaque or sign
- Pencils
- Sticky tape
- Eraser
- Ruler
- Printed copy of a suitable lettering style

1. Preparation

In this project, we will work through the stages for making a simple house sign using calligraphy and some basic decorative motifs. These basic principles can then be adapted as you develop your own style and crafting skills.

As with many other blanks used in these projects, plaques and signs are very easy to get ahold of from a range of art and craft suppliers. They are often available in birch plywood, which can be a cheaper option than solid wood blanks. Watch out for shaped MDF blanks and avoid purchasing them in error—they give off fumes when heat is applied to them. Plaque blanks can be purchased in a range of shapes, including square, rectangular, oval, octagonal, and many more. The larger or more ornate signs often have decorative shaped edging formed by routing. It is also possible to buy rustic natural-edged plaques that look like a slice of tree trunk, complete with the bark edging: these signs look stunning in a rustic setting, such as on a cottage or a farm gate.

Once you have bought the shape and style of sign you require, you will need to consider where it will be displayed and how it will be fitted. Some plaque blanks are sold with pre-drilled holes for fitting purposes, but you may have to make your own if the sign does not already have them. If the sign will be held in place with screws, it is best to plan where the holes will need to be drilled at the beginning so you do not ruin part of your pyrography design later on. The other alternative for larger signs is to fit a pair of metal brackets onto the reverse with small screws, which has the advantage of not affecting the side you will be decorating: this is my preferred method for fixing signs. I prepared the surface of the sign by rubbing it lightly with fine sandpaper and then using a soft cloth to get rid of the remaining dust and loose particles.

Blank wooden signs are available in a wide range of sizes and shapes to suit any purpose.

2. Plan Your Design

Once you have decided how the sign will be held in place and made any necessary adjustments, it is time to start planning your design. The lettering will be the focus of the design and will need to be as big as possible so it can be read from a reasonable distance. Decide what text you need to have on the sign. Does the house concerned have a name? Does it just have a number? Do you want to include the street name, or perhaps the surname of the family that lives there? Does the sign have a different purpose and need a message to reflect that instead, such as a warning about the family dog? Remember to make sure the details are accurate with no spelling mistakes at the earliest stage possible. The example I have created for this project uses a house name, as completing blocks of text is generally more complex than a number alone.

You will also need to plan any decorative designs or images you wish to include on the sign. Consider the size of these elements and where they will be located on the surface. Will you use a decorative border running around the edge? Do you want to include an image that relates to the text in some way? Or is there another reason for the chosen design, such as a favorite animal or flower selected by the family members who live at the house?

Use the plaque to plan how large the lettering will be, and where you will place any images. If you are using a tracing method to recreate the text, you can experiment with copying the text on a photocopier or on your computer to adjust the size. I chose to draw the lettering by hand, so I'll show you the process I went through to mark up the plaque and construct the letters that way. To create the calligraphic lettering in this design, we will draw it out using the double pencil method described earlier in this chapter. Whether you're tracing or freehanding the elements of the sign, the important thing is that by this point you should have decided where everything is fitting on the blank.

3. Draw the Guidelines

My plaque will include two words to form the name of a house: "Oak Cottage." Due to the shape of the plaque, these words will be placed one on top of the other, so I need to draw two identically sized pairs of parallel lines. As the lower case g has a descender, I will also need to leave sufficient space under the lowest set of lines to accommodate that. I want to use as much of the plaque as I can so that the name of the house is as visible as possible to any visitors.

Use a pencil and ruler to draw out your lines, and measure carefully to ensure they are parallel and accurately placed. The paired lines I drew

Oak Cottage

This is the Gothic calligraphy font that I will use in this project. The red squares at the edge indicate the nib widths so that you can establish the proportions of the upper and lower case letters.

were both 2¾" (70mm) apart. Because the first word, "Oak," is shorter, it does not matter that the curve of the sign reduces the amount of space available for the first pair of parallel lines. I will place the word centrally to make the layout more attractive to the eye and use the space in the most appropriate way possible.

Once the tramlines have been drawn, you will need to set up a two pencil–calligraphy tool to map out your calligraphy letters (see page 121). If you are using a calligraphy book to guide you, choose a font and remember to check the relevant nib widths: these will indicate the proportion of the letters. For example, the font I am using is based on capital letters that are seven nib widths in height and lower case letter that are five nib widths high. The nib widths can often be

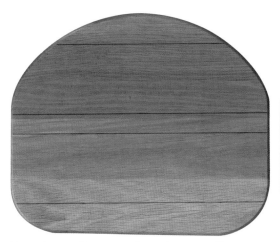

Draw the tramlines to mark out the top and bottom edges of the capital letters.

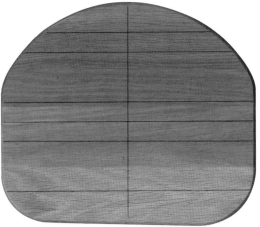

Add a vertical center line to help you balance the design, as well as the third tramline to show the height of the lower case letters.

indicated by a stack of blocks at the side of a calligraphic alphabet, as pictured on page 129.

Divide the distance between the tramlines equally in relation to the required height of the capital letters. In my case, the tramlines were 2¾" (70mm) apart and the capital letters need to be seven nib widths high: this means that the width of my pencil "nib" must be ⅜" (10mm) across. You can then work out that the lower case letters (at five nib widths) will be 2" (50mm) in height.

Draw in a parallel line at the correct height within the tramlines to mark the limit of the lower case letters. The lines are vital to ensure your letters remain correctly in proportion as you construct them. I also added a vertical center line for reference, in order to help me balance the letters and assist with the layout.

Use two pencils taped together to draw out the calligraphy lettering. Keep looking at the source example. Redraw areas if you are not satisfied with the initial drawings.

4. Draw the Design

You now need to tape your two pencils together so that the sharp points of the lead are the correct distance to form your required nib width. This can take a little bit of trial and error to get right: you may need to tape the pencils to another item to get the correct distance or place something between them to hold them apart. To achieve my calligraphy nib, I placed two folded pieces of card between the two and then taped them together firmly. The extra card was thick enough to hold the other two pencils apart to form a gap exactly ⅜" (10mm) between the points.

You are now ready to start drawing out the calligraphy letters, as per the tips given earlier in this chapter. Hold the pencils at the angle required to form thick and thin strokes depending on the direction in which they move. Refer to your chosen alphabet frequently to make sure you are forming the letters correctly. Remember to leave sufficient space between each letter so they do not appear cramped.

If you are not happy with the layout of your letters at first, simply erase them and start again, making necessary adjustments to prevent the problem from reoccurring. Spending more time at the planning stage will save you wasting both time and materials by using the pyrography pen too early. It doesn't matter too much if your pencil lines are a little wobbly, as these can be tidied up when you burn: they are only there to provide you with a rough indication of the letter structure.

Once you have finished drawing the letters onto the surface, prop the plaque up and look at it from a distance to check that you are happy with the composition. Taking a step back can help you to view the design in a more objective light—try to imagine the finished effect as you study it.

Use a bladed nib or similar to create the crisp outlines of each letter.

Erase the remaining pencil construction lines and shade the narrowest areas of each letter using the edge of a spoon point nib or similar.

5. Burn the Outlines

You are now ready to start burning. Select which nib you want to use to draw the outlines of your letters. If the letters are quite large, you could choose a bladed nib to help create the crisp straight lines and smooth curves. You may feel more comfortable using a writing nib or the edge of a spoon point nib, which can be easier to move across the surface when making curved marks. Personal preference and comfort are the main considerations, and you will probably already be starting to get a feel for what you can achieve with different nibs by working through other projects and designs. I used a medium skew to complete my outlines: the length of the blade helps when forming the long straight lines and you can lift the skew slightly to use just the tip when working on curves.

Use a medium-high heat setting to create the outlines of each letter. Work steadily and carefully, particularly when creating the thinner lines of each letter.

Once all of the outlines are finished, rub out all remaining pencil marks with an eraser before you start to fill in the letters.

6. Create Tone

Now consider how you will fill the letters with shading. Filling them with a solid black tone will ensure the name of the house is clearly visible to any visitors. You may wish to use a different style of shading that fades from dark to light in certain directions and adds a more three-dimensional effect to the letters. You could also include decorative motifs inside the larger strokes if you wished. The choices are endless and you can make your own design decisions based on the appearance and feel you wish to create.

I started by using the fine edge of a spoon point nib to block in the narrowest areas of each letter, where the strokes were thin or two lines joined at an acute angle. This ensures the quality of the outline is not ruined by using a nib that is too large and goes over the lines in those places.

Choose a broader nib for filling the letters in with tone. This will help you to work across the necessary areas more quickly than with a fine detailed nib. Remember that you can always use shade along the edge of the outlines first to create the protective barrier that will help reduce the chance of you making a mistake on your sharp and detailed outlines.

In this example, I used the bowl of a spoon point nib at a medium-high temperature to create a protective border along each crisp outline. As well as ensuring I didn't go over the outlines in error, this dark edging was also an important part of the shading technique I used to create a textured three-dimensional effect.

Once the borders were complete, I used a ball point stylus on the same temperature setting to fill in the rest of the letters with a stippling motion. This created a nice textured appearance for the calligraphy letters.

Add the protective border to the inner edge of each outline so that you are less likely to make mistakes when blocking in.

Add a textural tone by stippling the remaining areas with a ball stylus nib.

If you wish to add any further decorative images or designs, draw them with pencil first to ensure you are happy with the proposed layout.

7. Add Adornment

When you have completed shading the letters to form the house name, you can further adorn the sign with any form of decoration that you wish. It is best to stick to bold designs in keeping with the large lettering used in the sign, and also because more delicate signs may suffer more when exposed to outdoor sunlight. Consider adding a motif that makes reference to the house name (such as an oak leaf or an acorn for my example) or adding a simple border to frame the lettering.

Draw the details on first so you can ensure you are satisfied with the layout before you start burning. You can draw the images on freehand if you feel confident doing so, or you may use examples from a design book or another source. Make sure you get the layout exactly how you want it before you use the pyrography machine. It is easy to overcrowd a house sign and ruin the impact of the lettering if the layout becomes crowded.

After I had arranged the decorative elements used here, I then used a bladed nib to burn the outlines before filling in the tone with a small spoon point nib. I took great care while completing this stage due to the size and nature of the images chosen.

8. Finish

Once the sign is complete, it will need to be coated with a suitable protective varnish to preserve it from the damaging effects of the elements. Tips on using these substances can be found in the Getting Started section at the start of the book. Remember to follow the instructions on the container closely.

Chapter 7

Portraits

Perhaps the most difficult skill to learn in any artistic field is the ability to depict a realistic portrait of a person or animal. The challenge is due to the number of factors that you need to consider when planning your design.

A good portrait will capture the physical likeness, personality, and emotions of the subject. You can practice sketching your own face with pencil and paper until you feel comfortable with the proportion, features, and characteristics of the human face.

The main point is to study what you can actually see in front of you and respond directly to the subject's visual qualities: portray how the surface appears to you personally. The distance and scale of the portrait may play a part in this consideration. A surface that appears textured when you are close to it may look extremely smooth from a further distance away. You may know that a surface is rough to the touch from past experience but it may look smooth on the subject in question. You are creating a visual representation so trust your eyes, and do not waste time or effort creating what you cannot see. If you follow this principle, you should be able to create almost any surface quality or texture that you could possibly encounter.

Portraits can be a very challenging task for any artist or craftsperson. In this example, I used a dark background to provide a contrast for the delicate shading and tones.

Preparation

If you are working on a portrait of a friend or family member, I would suggest you carry out a lot of research first. You will know the character and personality of the person so you may already have an idea about how you would like to portray them. If the portrait is being carried out at someone's request, find out what ideas or opinions they have on how they would like to be depicted. Are they a serious person? Do they have a jolly personality? Each of these factors will be important when you start to plan your portrait.

You may want to sketch the subject to get a feel for the form and features you will draw for the final portrait. If the subject has time, they may be able to pose for you as a live model. Otherwise, you may have to work from photographs taken on previous occasions as source material for your studies.

Digital cameras are an invaluable resource when it comes to planning a pyrography portrait. You can spend time with the subject taking pictures from a range of angles and in a number of positions. Get them to wear a number of their favorite outfits if they cannot decide which one they want to be immortalized in. Encourage them to demonstrate a range of facial expressions from happy to sad, serious to laughing, and everything between. You can then spend time reviewing the results of the session on your home computer with the subject, deciding which image to work from.

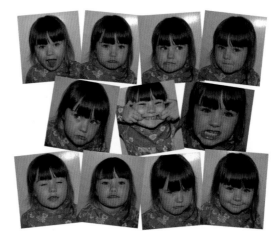

Take as many photographs of your subject as possible if you are able to arrange the time. You can use this session to capture a range of facial expressions and emotions, giving you choices for the expression to use in your pyrography design.

Animals

You can also carry out these photographic sessions with animals. I'll warn you now that they can be very unpredictable, as most pets are not particularly keen on posing for any period of time. The best way to capture animals on camera is often just by taking pictures as they are sitting, walking, playing, or resting naturally, though they may not respond too well to a camera repeatedly pointed in their face! You can always trawl through family photograph albums for previous pictures if you need more inspiration.

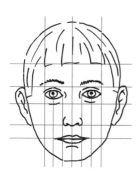

Paying attention to the proportions relative to each feature is essential.

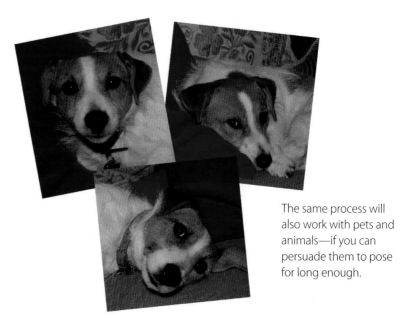

The same process will also work with pets and animals—if you can persuade them to pose for long enough.

Tracing the Structure

Drawing faces freehand is a challenge and something that even the most artistic people can struggle with when it come to capturing a certain expression or appearance. As the preparation of the image structure is vitally important in pyrography, tracing an image will save you a lot of wasted time and effort while also ensuring you will be satisfied with the composition of the design.

Once you have chosen the best photograph or image for the portrait, you will need to work out the size you need to work at based on the wooden item into which you are planning to burn. Again,

When tracing a portrait, start by drawing the concrete details such as the jaw, nose, ears, lips, teeth, spectacles, and any other linear features.

The next step is to draw any shadow lines or areas, made up by darker sections of tone that do not necessarily have a hard or defined edge.

the capabilities of the computer allow you to resize the digital image and print it at the required size for you to refer to.

My personal recommendation would be to print the image twice, once normally and once in reverse: remember that tracing from a mirror image cuts out one of the stages in the transferring process. You can use the normal print to refer to when burning the design onto the wood.

When copying the portrait onto the tracing paper, you do not want to waste too much time by tracing every minute detail. The aim of tracing is to record as much information as required to give yourself a good basis to work from with the pyrography pen.

Look for the key features and areas from the portrait you are copying. Start with what I call the concrete details, namely the structural lines that form the face. These would include the jaw line, nose, ears, lips, teeth, spectacles, jewelry, and any other linear feature.

I would then move on to tracing the outline of any distinctive shadow features: this might include the shadow cast by nostrils, dimples, eyelids, inside the ears, and underneath the chin. These features may not be as defined as the concrete details and may be formed by the fall of shadows or similar. This is also the point when you might record softer facial features such as eyebrows, moustaches, or similar. Such items do not have a strong outline and are better regarded as areas of tone or texture.

The next area I would consider would be any highlight features, namely any strong areas of light or lack of tonal detail. This would include the bridge of the nose or cheekbones if the light source used to record the photograph was strong enough. There may be no significant areas of highlight, so do not worry if you can't see any: the aim of this process is to record what you can see, so don't worry if there is nothing there that warrants drawing out.

The final area I look out for on a portrait is any information points that would assist the pyrography stage. This might include the line of a parting, change of hair direction, or any other facial feature that helps to break the image down in some way. These points will help you complete the construction of the image, so look for key points to assist you in mapping out the whole area involved.

By focusing on only the key features and areas when tracing a face, you save time in the early stages that is better spent during the burning process. The pencil marks will be covered as you burn, so you only need the minimum of information to provide a basic map to work on.

If you are working on a large portrait and are unable to print it at the required size to trace from, the grid method is a useful way to enlarge the image to the required dimensions, as first described on page 93. Print the reversed image from your computer after adjusting the dimensions to a specified proportion of the finished design (for example, print the image at 25% or 50% of the required size). Draw a grid of ¾" (2cm) squares in pencil on a piece of tracing paper and place this over the source image. Trace the key features and areas of tone as described in the paragraph to ensure you have sufficient detail to reproduce the image in full.

You will now need to draw a grid directly onto the wooden surface: work very lightly in pencil so that the lines can be erased easily. If you had printed the image for transfer at 50% of the required size, the squares on your new grid will need to be 1½" (4cm) across. If you had printed it at 25%, the new grid will need to have squares that are 3" (8cm) across. The new grid should have exactly the same number of squares as the original if your calculations have been correct. Once the grid is in place, you can start to copy

the information across from your first traced grid square by square, so that you are left with an enlarged version of the key points from the smaller source image.

Whichever method you use to transfer your image of choice onto the wooden surface, you are ready to burn once the pencil has left the surface. If you have transferred over the basic details of the image but feel you need more structure before you start to use the pyrography pen, you can always draw freehand over the existing image and add more lines to help you understand what goes where.

Add any highlights next. Look for areas of the face that show the fall of strong light or similar. These may also be areas you do not want to burn at all, so they are important for successful completion of the design.

Finish by adding any other information points, such as hair partings, change of hair direction, and other facial features such as beauty marks. You are now ready to transfer the image to the wooden surface.

Building Up the Portrait

When I work on portraits or other tonal studies, I tend to work in the same way no matter what the subject is. I start with the darkest and boldest lines or areas, so I immediately start to define key areas and construct the image with the main points of reference. Many of the darkest areas will be shadows or other strongly defined areas of tone. Once you start to add these in, you will have started the process of mapping out the structure of the image.

Consider which pyrography nib you will use at each stage of the portrait's construction, as well as the temperature setting and the way you hold or apply the pen itself. Using an appropriate nib will ensure you make the most suitable mark for the required texture or effect.

Do not start by drawing an entire outline using an even solid line, as this may make your portrait look like a cartoon. Look at the image you are using for reference and you will see very few features appear to have a bold line around them. Most features are actually defined by the change of tone and the fall of light or shadow across their surface, so be sensitive to what you can see in front of you and try to recreate that as best as you can.

If you prefer, you can work in the opposite way to create a portrait, working through from the lightest areas to the darkest. Many of the earlier projects and exercises in the book were planned in that way, as it is often easier for a beginner learning pyrography to work up to the darker marks steadily. The way we work all comes down to personal preference, so make sure you work in the order that feels most comfortable and gives you the best results.

Facial Features

Facial features are very distinct and stand out against the more subtle tones of the skin and hair. As a result, they often contain a range of tone and detail in a comparatively small area of the actual portrait. Once the darkest areas have been added, the next step I move onto is to complete the visible facial features as units in their own right. This helps to build up the most important areas of the portrait as soon as possible, and allows you to then tailor the rest of the portrait to match in with them accordingly. Each facial feature has its own requirements in the way they are depicted, and the success of the portrait is dependent on the way that you portray them.

The facial features of animals can be even more complex than those of humans. Whether you are drawing the folds around a dog's mouth, the structure of a cat's ear, or any other feature, each will have their own structure, texture, and changes of tone you will need to be sensitive toward in order to recreate them realistically. If you have any concerns about tackling facial features, practice drawing them first. You can try some pencil sketches on paper to build up your confidence, before moving on to some experiments on scrap wood with your pyrography machine if you wish. With time and practice, working on subjects such as these can become second nature. Follow the same steps described for any portrait: study the subject, sketch and practice if necessary, and then complete the design with constant reference to what you can physically see.

Eyes

Eyes are complex due to the combination of extreme tones, from dark pupils to the white areas around the iris. You also need to consider the folds of the lids, the soft lines of the eyelashes, and the delicate shading of the iris itself. Eyes are almost always my first port of call due to their importance.

STEP-BY-STEP GUIDE: HINTS FOR DRAWING EYES

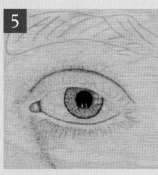

1 The eye is a very demanding and challenging subject, and possibly the most important part of a portrait.

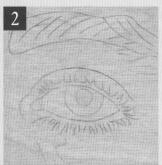

2 Trace or draw the main structure of the eye lightly with a pencil onto your wooden surface.

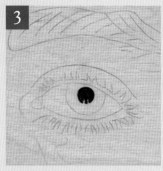

3 Start by adding the darkest part of the eye, the pupil, with a shading nib. Remember to look carefully for any reflections or light as you can leave these blank: this will help to make the eye look as realistic as possible.

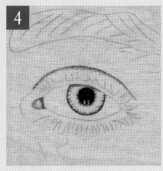

4 Start to build up the next darkest shadow areas. I shaded the fold above the eyelid and the corner. I started shading the edge of the iris to form the delicate patterning of the colored ring.

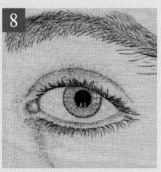

5 I then softly shaded the remaining section of the iris with a shading nib before adding some extra definition by shading around the eye with the nib set to a low temperature. Keep the nib moving across the surface constantly to avoid any scorch marks that may ruin the soft tones.

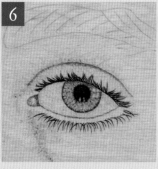

6 A bladed nib was used in a light flicking motion to create the dark eyelash hairs.

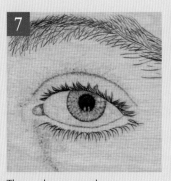

7 The eyebrow was then completed in a similar way to the eyelashes, creating a crosshatched network of lines to form the area required. The lines are closer together and more densely packed in some areas to give the impression of more hair as accurately as possible.

8 I then worked back over the whole image to make sure the tonal balance appeared correct, adding more shading where needed to increase the sense of definition and form.

Nose

The nose can be very difficult to portray accurately. The only strong tonal change is found at the nostrils, which are usually areas of darkest shadow. The actual outline of the nose can sometimes be apparent only as a subtle change of skin tone against the cheek, depending on the angle of the face. Portraits composed at a slight angle help to define the nose by creating a stronger shadow against the eye socket and cheek, when compared to a portrait where the subject is facing the viewer head on.

STEP-BY-STEP GUIDE: HINTS FOR DRAWING NOSES

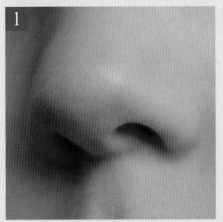

1

Noses are difficult to portray accurately as they have very few defined lines other than the edge of the nostrils.

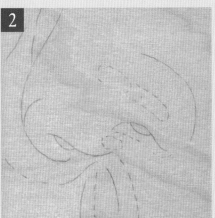

2

Trace or draw the main structure of the nose lightly with a pencil onto your wooden surface when constructing the portrait. Mark key areas of shadow and tone to assist with defining the shape.

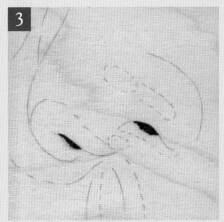

3

Start by shading the darkest areas of tone, which is the inside of the nostrils. I used the edge of a spoon point nib on a medium temperature.

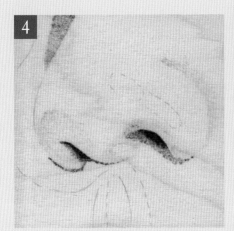

4

I turned the temperature down slightly and started to add the shadow around the edge of the nostrils and down the far side of the nose. I then used a low temperature to start adding skin tone and build up the impression of the form.

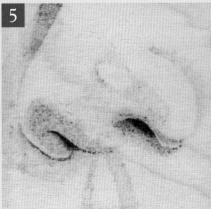

5

I worked back over the shaded areas carefully to build up the intensity of the tone where necessary. If you work carefully and slowly, you can create subtle blends of tone with smooth changes. Remember to leave any areas of highlights completely free of burning as well.

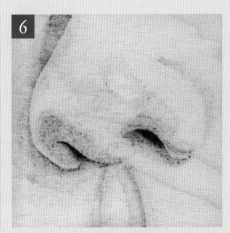

6

I added very soft shading along the edges that were in shadow to define the soft shape of the nose, as well as the soft ridges leading toward the mouth.

Mouth

The mouth is another area that takes time and effort in order to guarantee a successful portrait. Drawing a mouth involves depicting hard surfaces (teeth) against softer textures (lips). The change in tone between the lips and the face can be very soft and subtle, so a great deal of attention needs to be paid to getting the balance right. There is no outline that defines the lips, so sensitive use of shading and changes of tone must be used to illustrate the mouth accurately and realistically.

STEP-BY-STEP GUIDE: HINTS FOR DRAWING MOUTHS

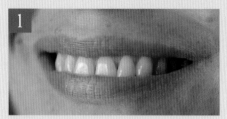

Constructing a mouth in a portrait often requires successfully combining the hard linear structures of the teeth with the soft forms of the surrounding lips.

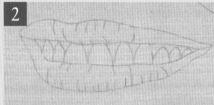

Trace or draw the main structure of the mouth lightly with a pencil onto your wooden surface when constructing the portrait.

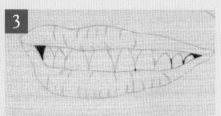

Shade the darkest areas first using a fine nib. If the mouth is not open, there may be no areas of dark shadow at all.

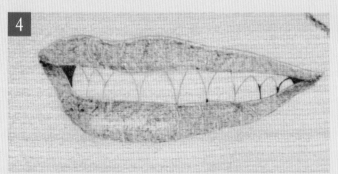

I used a spoon point nib on a low to medium setting, moving in a soft circular motion to shade the lips and add the form of the muscles. The tone can be added sensitively to define any areas of shadow. You can also leave areas free of shading for highlights.

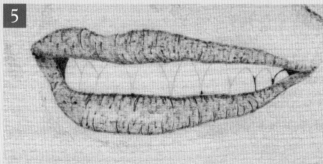

Lips are covered with soft creases that can be used to define their curved forms. These were added softly using a spoon point nib on a slightly increased temperature. I also started adding the delicate skin shading around the mouth on a low temperature.

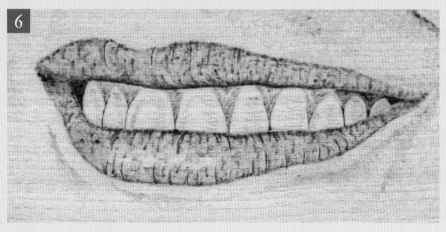

I finished off by shading the teeth and gums, using fine lines where the teeth met and shading the gums as sensitively as possible to create the sense of their form. I then completed the shading around the mouth to ensure the tonal balance was correct and appropriate to define the shape.

Ears

Ears are complex forms to depict and require a sensitive approach. Often an ear is partially covered or surrounded by hair, which helps you to define its shape. The soft curves and folds inside the ear itself require delicate and subtle blending to portray them accordingly.

STEP-BY-STEP GUIDE: HINTS FOR DRAWING EARS

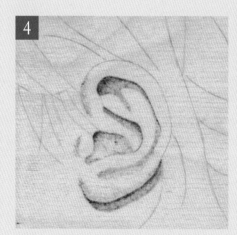

1

Ears can be difficult to portray accurately due to the complex nature of their folds and curves.

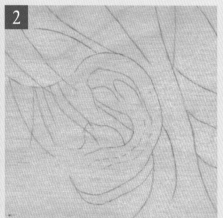

2

Trace or draw the main structure of the ear lightly with a pencil onto your wooden surface when constructing the portrait. Remember to study how the ear affects the hair around it if necessary.

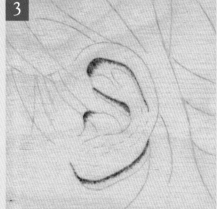

3

Start by softly shading the darkest areas of shadow. I used the bowl of a spoon point nib and kept the nib moving softly to ensure no harsh lines were created where they were not evident in the image.

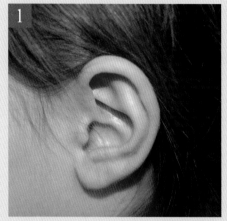

4

Reduce the temperature and start to create a blended tone, moving from the darkest shadows into the mid-tones. Try to ensure the changes in tone are smooth and gradual to emphasize the soft flowing forms of the ear itself.

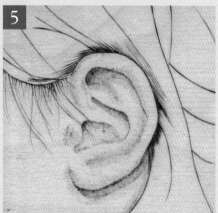

5

The hair around the ear may also move across in front of it if long enough. You can create the delicate lines of the hair using a bladed nib in a flowing movement.

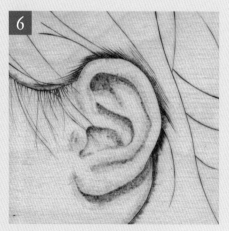

6

Work over the areas of shade until you are satisfied with the result. The shadows should not be too dark or too light, as either of these will make the image look too flat or stylized. A smooth transition of tone will give you the most successful results.

Hair, Longer Fur, and Feathers

Hair provides a challenge for the pyrographer. While skin can often be viewed as a smooth surface, hair has length, shape and direction to consider: the success of your design will depend on how well you can represent the surface through mark-making. The way you approach hair in your designs will be the same process if you wish to depict longer fur in an animal portrait, or feathers if you are drawing a bird.

Scale: The first issue to consider is the scale you are working at: the larger the scale, the more information you will be able to provide and record. If you are working on a large portrait of a bird, you will be more likely to see the structure of individual feathers and the way they are layered. If the image is being created at a smaller scale, the technique you use you portray the surface may be looser and more texturally based.

Considerations: There are a number of points to consider when you are about to work on an area of hair or similar. Start by studying your subject closely, whether it is a photograph or the person themselves. Consider the following questions as they will shape the way that you represent the hair in your portrait:

What color is the hair? The lines that you use to create the impression of dark hair may be more densely applied or thicker than those that you use for fair hair.

How does the color of the hair change across the image? Consider the effect of highlight and shadow on the hair, and how you will portray this.

How long is the hair you are trying to portray? To create a successful representation, the lines you use will need to match what you see on your subject.

Does the hair have an unusual shape or characteristics? For example, is the hair curly or frizzy in appearance? Has the hair been shaped into a ponytail or other style?

Which direction does it follow as it moves across the surface? As hair is usually laid over or protruding from a living surface, the direction that it follows helps to give you an idea of the three-dimensional form underneath.

Are there any special features to consider? Does the hair have any areas where it thins out or changes direction? Styled hair may have several layers that need to be completed carefully in order to build up the full appearance in your portrait. You may also need to depict hair accessories such as bands, pins, or barrettes.

When working on hair, fur, or feathers, it is best to use the finest nib or point you have available for your pyrography machine. Bladed nibs are ideal for creating the fine sharp lines needed to represent hair. Alternatively, you could use the edge of almost any shading nib to create fine lines. You may wish to consider re-shaping a nib using a small file, or by tapping the nib's edge with a hammer to make it thinner.

Make sure you do not select too high a temperature when making the marks for the hair: this may result in lines that are uneven and not consistent in thickness. Do not press too hard because the lines will lose their delicate and fluid shape. Use a light pressure as you move the nib smoothly across the surface of the wood.

When you start to work on an area of hair in a portrait, do not start by adding a solid outline around the whole area as this gives an unrealistic and unnatural appearance. Create a broken outline made up of individual hairs to give the impression of a soft surface made up of smaller structures. The lines you use do not have to be completely parallel: they may converge in places, move apart at an angle or even cross over. Using lines that do this will help recreate the natural and organic feel of a hairy surface.

If the area to be covered is quite large, add pencil lines for reference at regular intervals to help you map out the direction the hair should follow. Break the area down into sections if it makes it easier for you: this is a particularly useful way of working when constructing a portrait of a person with a specific hair style. Because a surface covered with hair is made up by numerous individual follicles, you will also build up the surface of your picture by using many different lines. It doesn't matter if one particular line is a little faint, as it will still work with the rest to form the textured surface. If you work lightly and carefully, you can take as much time as you need to build up the surface until you are satisfied with the result.

STEP-BY-STEP GUIDE: HINTS FOR DRAWING HAIR

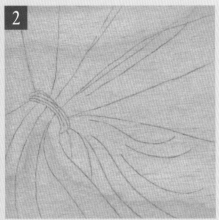

1 Hair can be a very difficult surface to portray accurately. Take time to study what you can see and how this forms the surface quality, texture, and appearance.

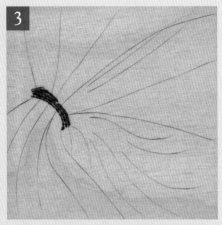

2 Using a pencil, trace or draw the main shapes made by the direction of the hair onto your wooden surface. Add as many lines as necessary as reference for the direction or flow that occurs.

3 Start by lightly burning over the pencil construction lines. I burned the hair band in using a ball stylus nib, as this also gives me a starting point to work from when creating the hair itself.

4 Use long flowing lines with a bladed nib such as a skew, following the direction of the hair as accurately as possible. Look carefully for areas where the sections of hair overlap or cross. Leave patches blank to represent highlights, allowing the surrounding lines to softly taper out as you approach them.

5 Turning the temperature up slightly will allow you to create darker lines for a sense of shadow. This effect can also be achieved by packing lines together very closely.

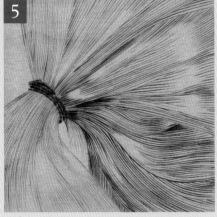

6 Work back over areas where the shadows are most obvious, adding additional lines to build up the sense of layers and depth. Continue this process until you are satisfied with the finished result.

Smooth Skin and Fur

Whether your subject is human or animal, the key feature of any portrait is that there will be a great deal of soft surface that you need to portray. This will include flesh or skin, usually in combination with some fur or hair. After completing the key features and dark areas of shadow, the next step to consider is generally hair and skin. These can be comprised of large expanses of surface area that need careful attention to complete in an appropriate way.

Flesh or skin is generally a very smooth surface texture with gradual changes in tone. The shading technique you select needs to reflect that if you want to achieve a realistic portrait. The areas of skin are often marked out most strikingly by the other physical features that surround or appear within them. I usually complete skin tones last when working on a portrait, so the key features are already finished and the skin texture is used to link each section together into one coherent and successful image. Smooth or glossy animal fur can be treated in the same way as skin, as often there is no visible difference to the eye of the viewer.

The best way to suggest skin tone in pyrography is to use a broad shading nib on a low temperature and build up the surface gradually. Start by covering the required area with the palest tone you will use and then slowly darken the areas that need it to suggest the fall of light or shadow across the form of the face. Each change in tone will need to be carried out patiently and blended as smoothly as possible so the surface appears to be soft and curved. The techniques you use will be no different to the initial shading and tonal exercises described in Chapter 2.

Pay careful attention to the areas where the skin or smooth fur meets other surrounding features such as fingernails or hair. Study the shape and the way areas fit together. Is there a defined line or is the join more subtle, such as a hairline? It is often more difficult to portray changes where the tones are very similar, such as fingernails or lips, so you will need to be sensitive to these areas and ensure you do not overwork or define them too heavily. Use untreated areas of wood as highlights to help define the shapes if there is a lack of shadow or line definition to assist you.

Once you have completed the hair and skin, check back to the subject and see if there are any final small details that need to be added to complete the portrait. If there are any skin blemishes such as freckles, birth marks, or similar, these are best added after the general skin tones have been completed, ensure they are visible in the finished image.

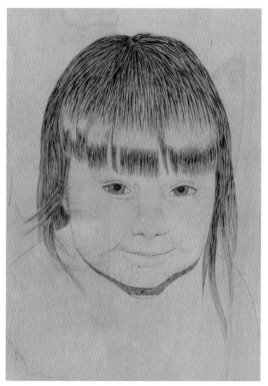

The face alone has been recreated in this portrait of my daughter. Children make great subjects that will really test your tonal abilities due to the soft and smooth texture of their skin.

Clothing and Accessories

Many portraits will need to include more than the face itself. The subject may be wearing spectacles or jewelry you wish to include in your design. You may want to include part of their body in the image. You may just choose the neck and shoulders, or you may wish to do a full body portrait at the other extreme.

If your portrait includes any clothing, the best approach is to treat it as a textured surface. If the clothing is too fussy or bold, the eye of the viewer may be distracted from the main focus of the portrait, namely the face itself. I often use a fade out technique as I reach the edge of a portrait, so the clothing is either completed with a softer, less distinct shading or just represented through lines alone. If you decide to portray the clothes realistically, they can essentially be regarded as a soft surface similar to skin, and will need to be represented with carefully blended tones

and shadows. The folds in the clothes will often give a range of tonal changes, from dark shadows to soft highlights.

Many people wear jewelry, spectacles, or other accessories that form part of their appearance and personality in exactly the same way as their physical features do. These need to be represented very sensitively to ensure the portrait is still successful. If a pair of earrings or spectacles are drawn in too heavily, they will not look right and will distort the balance of the portrait, detracting the attention from the face. My main tip would be to draw out the accessories carefully and ensure the proportions are correct. When you start burning, make sure you work lightly at first, gradually building up any areas of tone until you are satisfied the appearance is correct. It is not always easy to correct or amend problems that are too heavily burned, so a cautious approach is the best way forward. If your subject always wears a certain accessory, then the portrait may not be recognizable if the accessory looks wrong, regardless of how well you have constructed the face.

Final Details

When working on any of these fine details to complete a portrait, always remember to bear in mind the mark-making and textural experiments you have done before. You may recall a certain mark that perfectly portrays a certain facial feature. For example, the blush marks I described in Chapter 1, where a soft burn is made by holding a hot nib a few millimeters above the wooden surface, are useful for suggesting freckles.

If you do not wish to create a fully shaded torso, which may detract from the face itself, you can add subtle lines with minimal shading to hint at the body structure.

Finishing Touches

You may decide that your portrait needs a little something just to finish the design in the best way possible. There are a number of finishing touches you may want to consider.

Border: If the portrait has been added to a large wooden item or surface, it may look lost on its own with nothing to tie it in with the area surrounding it. Adding a border can be a simple yet effective way of finishing a portrait piece, as it will act as a frame for the image you have created. The border should be simple so it does not detract attention away from the main focus of the portrait itself. Make sure the border does not cramp the design or overpower it: the spacing between the border and the image is essential, as is the weight or thickness of the border itself. A dark border may make a delicately shaded portrait look insubstantial in comparison.

Personalizing: If you wish, you may want to add some text to the portrait, such as the name of the subject or details of the occasion to which it relates. As with borders, the font and style of lettering chosen will need to complement the tone of the portrait, rather than clash with it. We will look at making personalized gifts and the related considerations in Chapter 8.

Background: Adding a background is another way that you can finish a portrait design. It may be used to place the portrait in a certain situation or location relevant to the subject. You may wish to use a background from one of the research photographs you took or from another image entirely. The background may be a room, a garden, a landscape, or anything you like: it may just be an item on a tabletop such as a vase or plant pot. You can also invent the background completely, drawing it in freehand from your imagination. Choose a background that relates to the subject as it will place them in a familiar context: for example, an avid reader could be portrayed with a background of bookshelves.

A simple frame can turn a great portrait into a superb piece of artwork ready for display. You could also experiment with more elaborate borders if you wish.

As the portrait itself is the main attraction, do not include too much detail in the background you use or make it bolder than the subject itself. A good background should suggest a location or scenario and ground the image by placing it in a context, but it should not divert or sidetrack the viewer when they look at the item. Use light lines and tones wherever possible, and constantly compare what you are doing against the detail of the portrait itself.

Advanced: As you progress to more advanced portraits, you may find you will need to combine features from a range of sources to achieve the required results. Perhaps you would like to complete a portrait of two relatives who actually live on opposite sides of the world? Or you may find you would like to do a portrait of someone you know, but set in a different era of history. You can then become very creative in your planning. You may take elements from a photograph of a relative's face, a picture of someone in a certain costume, and an image of a faraway location. You would then be able to combine all of these elements to construct your own unique picture. If you cannot find a photograph of someone

I chose this portrait of my wife, as it was a beautiful pose and showed the real warmth of her character.

The finished portrait used the facial structure from the portrait combined with a cloak that I had drawn from scratch.

in a particular pose or outfit, see if you can find someone to model for you so that you can take your own photographs. This technique is particularly useful if you are not confident drawing the human body without reference.

I used a method like this to complete a portrait of my wife. I had a beautiful portrait photograph of her, but the background was very dark. It looked as if her face was floating because the clothes and surroundings could not be distinguished clearly. I wanted to create a portrait using the same facial position, but I decided to place the image into a more appealing scenario. I traced the main features of her face and head, but then researched various sources showing old-fashioned cloaks and capes. I eventually found an image of an elf princess in a hooded gown to inspire me. I traced my wife's face onto the wooden surface and then drew a cape freehand using the image of the princess for reference. This helped me to have more of an understanding in how the material of the cape would flow and fold, as well as where the clasp would sit. The finished portrait was very successful.

Working in Miniature

I often add small human or animal portraits to small wooden items such as key rings. Because the surfaces are generally no more than 2–2½" (5–6cm) in diameter, this can result in a conservative approach to mark-making that can still be very expressive. The purpose of the marks becomes more textural so the impression of fur is created. Moving the pyrography nib with a light flicking motion repeatedly across the surface builds up a soft furry texture or the appearance of hair. Turning the heat up slightly allows you to add some darker lines that look more solid when used to form shadows. Highlights are based on the sensitive use of the bare wood across the whole image. Using just three basic techniques to create shadow, highlight, and mid-tone can still lead to some really successful portrait designs: sometimes less is truly more!

Sensitive use of your pyrography nibs will mean you can create successful portraits, even on the smallest scale. Fur is a great surface to recreate in your designs, making animals fascinating subjects.

Practice!

Portraits are a popular subject across all artistic media, and pyrography is no exception. With time and practice, you will develop your confidence and skills in planning and completing portraits. As with any creative process, you will also build up your own personal style of expression to suit your preferred way of working. Feel free to practice as often as you can. There will be no shortage of photographs from family albums that you can use as the basis for your designs, and you may also make some great presents for relatives along the way! The processes described in this chapter for approaching a portrait form the basis for the way you can work for any realistic figurative design, so you can apply the same technique for realistic studies of other subjects such as hands, feet, plants, or manmade objects.

Recreating portraits in pyrography from photographs is a challenge but very rewarding. This pair of hair accessories was designed for a young girl who really loved her classic divas. I was especially pleased with the detail in the hairstyle of each famous iconic lady.

A cherished pet can be a part of your life for many years and is often regarded as a family member. Many people like to display pictures of their pets, both present and past, to recognize the special bond that develops. As a result, objects decorated with a portrait of a beloved animal friend are very desirable. Portraits in pyrography make a perfect gift for someone who wishes to celebrate their pet.

TOOLS & MATERIALS

- Photograph or other source
- Tracing paper
- Pencil
- Pyrography machine and tips
- Wood

1. Preparation

The first consideration when creating a pet portrait is the item to be decorated. A smaller item will mean the portrait may lack detail, while something that is too big may take far too long to decorate. It may also be sensible to stick to an item with a flat surface or a gentle curve at most. The most appropriate items for portrait work are generally plaques and plates, as they look perfect when displayed in the home. Most usually have a decorative shaped edge or lip, which gives the portrait a more finished appearance.

I was asked to do a portrait of a beautiful cat called Maude that, sadly, had passed away. It's always an honor to be asked to commemorate a treasured pet in this way, and I always aim to capture as much of the character of the animal as possible. I was sent a picture of Maude to work from, and the photograph that I was sent was absolutely perfect.

It is essential that the picture you work from be of a very good quality, as you will be aiming to transfer as much of the detail as possible. If the photo you try to work from is unclear or too small, you will be limited in what you can transfer over to your design. This photograph showed me that Maude had beautiful markings, which I wanted to portray as well as I could. She also definitely had the air of a typical cat about her: slightly aloof to all those around her and very relaxed.

A beautiful photograph of Maude, the cat.

2. Trace the Outline

Trace the key structures of the portrait from a copy of the original.

The next stage for me was to match the photograph with the item to be decorated. I had chosen a wooden sycamore plaque with a shaped edge, measuring 8" (20cm) in diameter. I enlarged the photograph on my computer so that it filled a page, to ensure the image of Maude was big enough to fill the plaque and not look too small.

I then traced off the main outlines of the photograph using tracing paper and a sharp pencil. Always make sure you trace from a reproduction of the photograph rather than the original, in order to avoid leaving pencil impressions behind.

It can be difficult to work out what to trace when making an image of an animal, especially when trying to reproduce fur or other soft surfaces. For the image of Maude, I traced the basic outline shape and then looked for other key areas to add definition. These included the eyes, the ears, the nose and muzzle, followed by key areas of fur where color change was very obvious.

Once you have traced the outline from the image, turn it over and draw the lines onto the reverse side, while leaning on a piece of scrap paper to avoid transferring the marks to your table or desk.

3. Transfer the Design to Wood

You can then turn the tracing paper back over to match the photograph and align it on your wooden plaque. Scribble lightly with a pencil over all lines to transfer the design softly onto the wood. If you need to add any lettering or text to the design, remember to leave adequate room for it at this point. I marked out two parallel tramlines in pencil before adding the traced design so that I left the right amount of space for a name to be added.

Mark out your lettering in pencil and you should now have a finished rough layout. If creating the item for a customer or friend, this is a good point to show the design to them for approval before you start burning: this ensures they are satisfied with the design and also reduces the chance of you making a permanent mistake. It would be horrendous if you spent hours creating a portrait only to find you had spelled the cat's name wrong!

4. Burn the Lettering

Once the layout has been approved, you are able to start burning. I decided to create the whole design using only the versatile spoon-point nib. The edge can be used to create distinct lines, while the bowl side is perfect for softer areas of shading. It is possible to create a variety of marks with only one such nib if you are sensitive to the way you apply it to the wood and the heat settings you use. It also saves you a lot of time by cutting out the need to let nibs cool and change them over frequently.

My technique is to start at the most defined or solid areas of the design and work downward to the softest or lightest areas. On this design, the obvious starting point for me was the lettering. I used the edge of a spoon-point nib to give me a nice clean line for the narrow italic lettering.

Transfer the basic portrait structure onto the plaque and draw out any lettering that is required.

Construct the lettering with a fine nib and then shade it.

5. Burn the Darkest Areas

Once you have completed the lettering, the next step is to find the most solid area on the animal image itself to use as a starting point. I started by transferring the darkest areas of the eyes, nose, and ears. I set the pyrography machine to a medium-high heat and used the edge of the spoon-point nib for the defined edges of the eyes. I then turned the spoon point over to use the bowl-shaped side to burn the dark areas with softer edges, namely the shadow areas around the eyes. Finally, I turned the temperature down and burned the subtle shadow of the nose using the spoon-point edge again. I then used the bowl edge to add the subtle color to the eyes themselves, leaving some areas untouched to show where the light reflects on the eyeball.

I added the dark shading to the edge of the ears, using a medium-high heat setting and the edge of the spoon-point nib. I used small strokes in the direction of the fur. I also decided to draw on the whiskers and long eyebrow hairs that were evident on the photograph. I had left these off initially as it would have made the image for transfer too crowded and possibly confusing. I added them on now so that I could work to try and define them in the portrait in two ways: highlighting them with marks or highlighting them by leaving them free of marks.

The next stage was to start building up the darkest areas of Maude's fur markings. After looking at the photo, I started at the areas around the eyes and ears to build on and out from the areas I had already completed. Using a medium-high heat setting, I continued to use small strokes with the sharp edge of the nib. This allowed me to create the top of Maude's head in a softer way with many vertical lines, rather than defining it with one horizontal line.

I then added some soft short lines on the back of her ear to give it a velvety appearance. The next step was to add the dark fur patches around her eyes: you can also see that this is where I

started to define her eyebrows by leaving them blank and working around them.

I then started to block in some of the larger darker areas of fur, using the bowl of the nib on a medium to high heat. I used a dotting motion, frequently lifting and applying the nib, to create a soft dappled effect. You can build up the darkness of the mark gradually, rather than pressing hard and scorching the wood beyond repair. Remember to pay attention to any areas you are leaving blank: you can see that the eyebrow hairs now stand out quite clearly from the dark fur, as they do in the original photograph.

Start by adding the darkest and most solid areas of the portrait. Use the edge of a spoon point nib sensitively to give the impression of a soft surface. You can also draw in any additional details before you start to burn in the areas concerned.

Complete the darkest patches of the fur, using the pyrography pen in small strokes to give a textured feel appropriate to the surface you are depicting.

6. Create Texture

The next stage was to finish off the crown on the top of Maude's head, where her fur was clearly a combination of black, brown and grey. I turned the machine down to a medium setting and used the edge of the nib in a series of small strokes to recreate the feel of fur. Work in the direction the fur takes on the photograph for a realistic effect: this was generally radiating out from the nose. Do not use a solid line for the edge of the head. I had now created a soft mottled representation of the markings on the top of Maude's head, and had also started to work down toward the long fur on her back. I had used longer strokes for this to demonstrate we could see the fur curling up and away from us, rather than looking straight at it like the markings on her face.

7. Add Details to Face

I finished Maude's ears to complete the top of her head. I turned the machine down to a low-medium setting in order to create the delicate ear hairs common to all cats. I used long slow strokes to create a network of delicate lines, constantly referring back to the photograph. I then used the bowl area in small circular motions to create the soft shading on the inside of each ear, spending more time in areas that I wanted slightly darker.

I decided to finish the face at this point, as it is clearly the most important part of any portrait. Using the same low-medium setting, I started to add delicate dots or small lines to complete the soft definition to the white areas around Maude's nose, mouth, cheeks, and chin. You do not want to make this area look too dark. The dots and marks need to be quite concentrated in areas such as the inverted Y-shape of the mouth, but lightly used on the fur itself. Keep referring back to the photograph if you need to check how you are getting on. I also used the edge of the nib to create some delicate lines that defined the whiskers past the edge of Maude's face.

Continue to give the portrait a soft, velvety feel as you work to add the mid-tone fur. Use short, straight strokes or a stippling motion to create this effect. The eyebrow hairs are now quite apparent as thin highlights through the shaded areas.

Use a lower temperature setting to create the delicate fine lines and detail of the ears.

Add the remaining soft definition to the cat's face by using light dots and marks. Add very fine lines for the whiskers.

8. Complete the Body

The next stage was to move onto defining the shoulder, body, and leg areas evident on the photograph. I turned the machine down to a low setting and used the bowl of the nib to create a very soft and subtle shading area on her chest, using small circular movements to gradually cover it as required. You can see this produces a slight discoloration on the wood without making distinct marks: ideal for shading a white area in a very subtle way.

I then turned the machine up to a medium-high setting and used a dotted irregular line with the edge of the nib to mark the left hand side of the neck and body. I then shaded in the dark area to depict the cushion Maude was resting on, using the same dappled technique with the bowl I used to create the darker areas on her forehead.

I used the bowl of the nib on a medium setting to add a little more direction and definition to the white fur on Maude's neck and under her chin. I then turned it up to a medium-high setting and created the body and leg area using both the bowl and edge of the nib. The direction of the fur was more apparent on the photo in this area, so remember to use strokes in the required direction. I used very dark marks to add shadow and represent the black fur, mixing in some smaller strokes with the edge of the nib to show the grey and brown areas for contrast.

Start to build up the shoulders and body area in keeping with the rest of the portrait. Keep referring to the photograph to make sure the balance of tone is correct.

Use a soft flicking motion to create the long hair around the neck and shoulders, giving the fur a more definite length and direction. Use a combination of mid-tone and darker marks to break up the surface and create a feeling of form and shadow.

9. Add the Finishing Details

At this point, the portrait is almost finished and it is usually best to compare it to the photograph to check if all shading is satisfactory. I decided I needed to add a little more shading to define the white neck area directly under Maude's chin, which now looked a little flat compared to the rich texture surrounding it.

I then burned a dark line on one lip of the shaped plaque edge, using the bowl of the nib on a medium-high setting. This is a useful way to add a shadow or border to tie the image down and finish it off.

The same technique of working can be used for any portrait, whether human or animal. Start with the solid, dark or most defined areas and gradually work down through the tones. It is always easier to make a light area darker, but not as easy to make something lighter once you have burned it into the surface. Practice makes perfect!

Chapter 8

Ideas and Inspiration

As your ambition and confidence grows in using your newfound

skills in pyrography, you will undoubtedly wish to explore

new avenues for potential designs and creations. Any artistic

media will lend itself to different avenues of creativity, many

of which will be shaped or influenced by your own individual

tastes or preferences. There are many sources you can look to

for inspiration, and this chapter documents some of the themes

and options that have provided me with ideas to use in my

work. This is not an exhaustive list by any means and you must

always be receptive to potential sources of inspiration, which

can crop up on you at any time.

I decorated this turned wooden goblet using a number of different techniques combined with the pyrography. I stained areas of the wood with colored inks, engraved textures into the surface with a rotary power tool, and added brass upholstery pins for contrast.

Color

Most traditional pyrography work demonstrates the application of heat to a surface so that the finished piece is created through the tone of the wood and the effects of the heat on that item. Some pyrographers are content to work wholly in this way, while others are keen to experiment with the use of color to enrich the palette and build on the tones available through burning. Color can be used to add a richness and depth to a design that would not be possible with pyrography alone. Too much color can ruin or detract from a pyrography design if it covers the natural qualities and appearance of the wood itself. If you completely disguise the wood, then you might as well be working on a piece of paper. Sensitive and delicate use of color can emphasize the qualities of both the wood itself and the marks you make upon it.

The way that color can be used in your pyrography design is influenced and controlled by the surface you are working on. Darker woods may not accept the use of some colored media in the same way a paler surface would. I would also recommend you complete the pyrography process first before you start to add any form of colored material: the area of color may become discolored when the heat is applied and, more importantly, the pigment or material that you apply may release harmful fumes when heated. You can treat the pyrography work as the outline for you to work inside and around, similar to a child's coloring book.

Whenever you decide to try any colored media with your pyrography work, try the material out on a scrap piece of wood first so that you can see how it handles and what it looks like. This will save you a lot of unnecessary wasted time trying to remove something that did not work properly. Make a few marks on the wood with your pyrography pen so that you can see how the color reacts when it is placed over or around the lines.

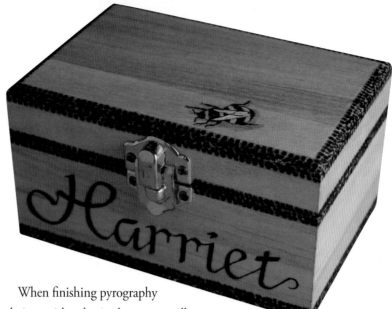

This personalized trinket box was decorated with a small bee design in pyrography, which was then colored using thinned acrylic paint.

When finishing pyrography designs with color in them, you will also need to check that the varnish or treatment you use does not distort or destroy the colors in any way. Using a wet varnish with a brush can reactivate a pigment and cause it to move from where it was originally applied, resulting in unwanted bleeding or muddiness. Using a spray varnish means you are not moving and disrupting the pigment on the surface. Your local art supply store will stock a range of varnishes and will be able to offer advice on suitability if you are not certain. Carry out test runs on scrap wood first. For the sake of a few minutes of extra effort, you may save yourself from ruining hours and hours of patient craftwork.

Paints

There are a variety of paints that can be used with your pyrography. Each type of paint has its own benefits and drawbacks when used in this way, and some are best left alone as they are not appropriate for combination with pyrography.

The burned wooden areas are not absorbent to paint and other liquids, which can be very useful. The paint will tend to run off the burned lines and marks, or work around them. This will work to your advantage as the paint will not obscure or cover the pyrography marks you have spent time creating. This can mean that the paint pools in the area without drying fully: make sure

Dry-brushing is a very useful technique for adding highlights.

Acrylic paints are thicker and can be used to give a more solid area of color that obscures the surface qualities of the wood below. They can be used to create quite bold and vivid areas of color, so they are particularly suitable for designs aimed at children. Acrylic paints are versatile and can be used quite thickly straight from the tube or watered down slightly to create a wash effect. This flexibility means you can create a range of color depths and hues using just a limited number of colors. Using paints of a thicker consistency means you can add color on top of the pyrography marks if you wish. Acrylics can also be used with a dry-brush technique: paint is added in small amounts to the brush and gently drawn across a textured surface, leaving a residue of the color on the higher points. Acrylic paints are perfect for blending and mixing so that you can create your own individual palette.

Oil paints are not well suited for use on wood with pyrography. Oil paints take a very long time to dry and the oil in them can bleed into the wood, discoloring the areas surrounding the paint.

Colored pencils

On very pale woods such as sycamore and birch, I have found colored pencils are useful to apply color to small designs. It is best to use the flat edge of the pencil to shade the color softly, rather than using the point, as this can result in a scratchy, lined area of tone. Because the pencils are designed for use on white paper or similar, the effect they give when used on wood can be quite understated and subdued. Colored pencils need a smooth and plain surface to be successful, so they are not ideal for woods with a distinctive grain or figure. If the wood has a strong figure, this can result in a rippled surface that rises and dips: using a pencil on such a surface will result in a streaky finish. On the plus side, they are easy to get hold of in most art supply stores and are generally cheap to purchase.

I used pencils in two different tones of purple/pink to give the color more depth and warmth. Using the pencils lightly to shade the fob also let the figure of the wood show through slightly.

you do not tilt the wood if there is still an excess of wet paint. The paint may run unpredictably and cover areas of the design you wanted to remain blank. To prevent this, allow the painting to dry and then gently dab the whole surface with an absorbent cloth or tissue to remove any unwanted traces still remaining.

Watercolor paints are quite transparent and allow the natural figure of the wood to show through. The colors are softer as a result. Due to their translucent quality, watercolor paints are only suitable for use on the palest of woods. The color would be too distorted by the underlying surface tone on darker woods. They can be very effective for subtle color highlights on detailed figurative designs. Watercolors are a good example of a thin paint that will allow pyrography marks to show through. This means you can be a little more liberal when applying them to a surface, as the watercolor paint will not dry on the pyrography marks and can be patted away gently with a soft cloth as previously described.

STEP-BY-STEP GUIDE: USING ACRYLIC PAINTS WITH PYROGRAPHY

When you study an area of hair closely, you will see there are many different tones and colors involved, along with areas of shadow and highlight.

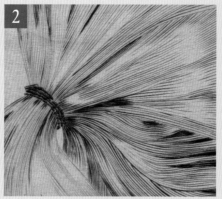

I used the pyrography study of the hair completed on a wooden tile in Chapter 7, which I wanted to add more realism and depth to by using color.

I started by adding a thin orange-brown wash of acrylic paint as a base coat for the lighter areas of hair.

I then added another thinned wash of dark brown paint for the base color of the darker areas.

Add a dark brown wash across the orange-brown layer to build up a sense of shadow and color change.

A slightly thicker wash of dark brown paint can then be added to the darkest shadow areas for definition.

A deep red-brown wash across the whole area adds warmth to the image and starts to pull each section of the image into one whole design.

Watercolor pencils

Watercolor pencils are used in a similar way to normal pencils, but you can then blend the tones gently with a small amount of water on a paintbrush. This creates a softer appearance and allows for subtle blended mixes. Try not to overload the brush with water, as this will saturate the wood and may allow the color to bleed slightly. The less water you can use, the better, even if you have to frequently dip the brush while working over an area of color. You may need to be patient, but the finished effect will be better as a result. I recommend blending colors together softly, as this adds warmth and depth to the overall effect. The colors of individual pencils can be a little bland or artificial on their own. For example, adding a little extra yellow or blue to a green surface can make the surface appear more natural when blended, as it softens the artificial brightness of the single tone.

Inks

Colored inks combine the boldness of acrylics with the delicacy of watercolors. The colors are bright when applied to a surface, yet they also allow the figure of the wood to show through from underneath. You need to be very careful not to apply them too heavily, as they can bleed easily, and discolor the wood more clearly than watercolors. Inks can be very successful when used to add color to areas surrounded by substantial areas of burned wood, as this acts as a barrier to prevent bleeding and emphasizes the contrasting color of the inks.

Inks are particularly good for decorating pale woods due to their slightly transparent quality. Experiment on a scrap piece of the wood you plan to use first so you can test how well the inks react when applied to the surface.

Pens

You may also wish to experiment with the uses of ink pens in your pyrography designs, as there are many different types and styles available. It is very easy to control where pens are applied as they do not flow like liquid. They do require a smooth working surface though, as any ridges will attract more color and prevent the pen from evenly working into the surrounding valleys. Markers are not always the easiest to blend smoothly, so make sure you carry out some trials on scrap wood before you move onto your intended piece.

Stains and dyes

Most D.I.Y. stores stock a range of timber stains, dyes, waxes, and creams, which can be used to change the tone of wood as well as protect or preserve it. As they can be applied by use of rags, brushes, or sponges, it would be possible to use these substances in a more creative manner to enhance your designs. Obviously, each of these substances will have their own guidelines and instructions on the correct way to apply them as they can be harmful when not used in the correct manner. Make sure you obey any instructions in relation to ventilation and toxicity of the substance, and do not apply them to the wood before the pyrography to prevent harmful fumes.

This rose motif was added to the top of a flower press with a dark burned tone underneath to emphasize the design.

Using the point of a watercolor pencil can create a scratchy coverage of the surface. Use the flat edge of the pencil to create a softer layer of tone.

Cover the image with a foundation layer of the basic color for each section of the image. I used a basic red for the flower and a green color for the leaves.

Go over the first layer of pencil with a second layer in a similar color. I used a slightly darker red and green pencil: this blending creates a slightly warmer and less artificial appearance for the colors.

You can then use darker colors to add shadow and create depth in the image.

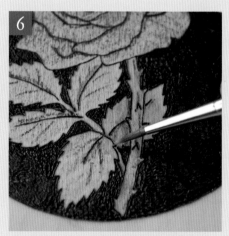

Use a fine paintbrush dipped into water to blend the pencil layers. Do not apply too much water as it may cause the colors to run or bleed.

The finished image will have warm, vivid colors with a soft blended look. You can also experiment with ways to add highlights or create more complex tone if you wish.

Personalizing

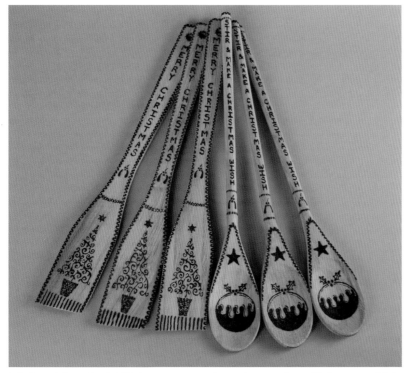

A commemorative gift is an item specifically made to celebrate a special occasion. This can include birthdays, engagements, weddings, anniversaries, graduations, baptisms, religious celebrations, commendations, personal achievements, or any other important event. Such an item may also be used as a tribute for a more solemn occasion, such as a memorial for a loved one who has passed away.

Any item created to commemorate an event will be unique. Such items cannot be bought off the shelf and therefore always have to be specially made. The item will always evoke memories of the event in question, which can create a strong emotional link for the person it belongs to. It will always have a meaning above and beyond its material appearance and value, due to the thought and effort that led to its creation.

Personalized gifts can be all shapes and sizes, and designed with any theme or style in mind. This miniature hairbrush with a festive theme makes the perfect Christmas stocking filler.

I designed these festive kitchen spoons and spatulas to sell at a Christmas craft fair. Gifts like these can be personalized with messages on the reverse to make them a long-lasting keepsake of a special occasion.

Lettering

One of the most important features of the commemorative design is the message it contains. This may include names, dates, personalized messages, poetry, song lyrics, and the like. The way the message is portrayed and depicted in the design is possibly the most essential element you will need to consider. Where is the text to be positioned? What size will the lettering be? What font will you use? How will the lettering suit the occasion?

The success of the whole design can hinge on the final question. The lettering needs to be appropriate in order to fulfil the design brief that you are working to.

When you are working on a design with several items of text, you may find it necessary to work in a number of fonts or sizes. Many of my wedding frames have included the name of the couple, the date of the big day and the venue for the ceremony. As the names are clearly the most important words, I use an ornate style of lettering to give the names the most visual impact. I select a similar font for the date and venue, or use my own handwriting: these details are then added at a smaller scale.

PEGGY & GILBERT
PEGGY & GILBERT
Peggy & Gilbert
Peggy & Gilbert
Peggy & Gilbert
Peggy & Gilbert
Peggy & Gilbert
Peggy & Gilbert

Try as many different fonts and lettering styles as possible to help you decide what will look best in the design you are planning.

Weddings

Many weddings have a theme you may be able to incorporate into your design to make it even more special. Carry out discrete research with relatives of the happy couple if the gift is a surprise. You may find out that a certain type of flower is being used in the bride's bouquet, or that a certain song will be used for their first dance at the reception. This may help you decide how to decorate an item, perhaps by using matching flower designs in a decorative border or incorporating significant song lyrics into the composition. Adding a personal touch in this way makes the item even more unique and guarantees the thought put into the item will be well received.

The most commonly requested commemorative gift I am asked to create is the photo frame. A beautifully decorated frame makes a fantastic gift as a photograph of the big event can be placed inside to complete the package.

Favors: As well as creating gifts for the happy couple, you may find the opportunity to use your pyrography skills to contribute to the wedding day as well. I have been contacted by couples who wish to add a handcrafted touch to their wedding reception. I have often been asked to make decorative wooden labels that have two functions: they act as the marker to show seating arrangements, and they also form a unique wedding favor that can be taken home as a memento of the happy occasion. If you drill a small hole in them, wooden tags can be attached to the napkin by ribbon: the hole can then be used afterwards to attach a key ring so that the guest can keep the item on a day-to-day basis. Working on a project like this can be very time-consuming and intense, but ultimately extremely rewarding due to the number of people that will see and keep your work. If each item features the same design, you may wish to experiment with ways to transfer them quickly to each tag, such as

This frame was made for a wedding in Ireland, so a bold Celtic pattern was selected with a matching font.

a stencil. Try and plan your design so it features a simple yet striking motif, something that you can easily repeat as required on each tag. Remember to make sure you take care over the spelling of each guest's name: get a typed guest list if you can so you have something to refer to.

You can use a wide range of other items for wedding favors if you don't want to use tags or fobs. Wooden napkin rings can be purchased at very reasonable prices from craft suppliers, and can easily be customized with a name and simple decorative design. Wooden thimbles may also be a suitable option. Many suppliers sell cut-out shapes made of birch plywood, so you may want to choose an appropriate shape for a wedding such as a heart, horseshoe, star, flower, or similar.

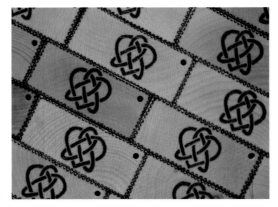

I made seventy matching table favors for a wedding in Scotland, each with an identical knotwork heart on the reverse and the guest's name on the front.

Personal touches

There are many ways that you can add a more personal touch to a design you are creating as a commissioned present on behalf of someone else.

I once created a decorative wooden plate for a family to give to their grandmother. I asked all members of the family giving the present to write or sign their names in pencil on the reverse with a personal dedication. I then burned over the handwriting with the pyrography machine to make them permanent. This worked particularly well for the writing of the children in the family, as it preserves a moment in their life forever: looking at the rear of the plate will always bring back memories of their relatives at a tender age, even when they have grown up and have families of their own.

You may also wish to use your pyrography skills to preserve other precious moments in time. A christening gift could include the silhouette of a newborn baby's hands or feet. It doesn't take long to draw around a hand or foot so that you can immortalize it in the design on a wooden surface. Such an image will again provide a talking point in the future, when the hand or foot concerned has grown to a considerably larger size!

Personalized frames can also be used to display other items such as newspaper articles, certificates, or medals: decorating the frame with a theme appropriate to the item contained within emphasizes the importance of the contents.

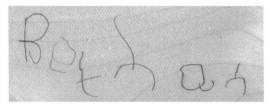

My young daughter was learning to write her name, so I gave her a piece of wood to practice on.

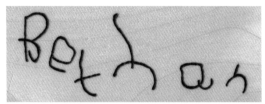

I was then able to burn over the lettering and make a permanent keepsake of her first attempts at writing.

Adding the details of a child's birth to the wooden bottle blank made this a unique memento to celebrate the latest addition to a family.

Capturing a moment in a child's life can be priceless. This coaster shows the exact size of a young girl's hand on a specific date. You could always consider designs that evolve with time, adding a new hand profile each year to visually show and capture the growth of the little person for many years to come.

A frame for an educational degree certificate may be decorated with a design relating to the subject matter that the study was in.

A decorative wooden box or chest also makes a nice commemorative gift. They can be used as treasure chests or memory boxes to store mementoes of a special occasion. There is something about human nature that makes many of us want to hoard precious items or little trinkets. As a result, boxes to keep our personal treasures in are just irresistible to some people! Such an item may be particularly suited as a gift to celebrate a birth or christening, as they can be used to protect and store important items such as the wristband of a newborn baby, their first shoes, photographs of the birth, cards from friends and relatives, and much more. The first precious moments of a new life can be kept safe for years to come in a beautiful box decorated by hand, adorned with the name of the child and their date of birth. A decorative handmade box makes a lovely present, particularly if the design is relevant or personal to the recipient in some way. It is very easy for a pyrographer to create a box that features someone's favorite animal, flower or other meaningful subject.

Humor

I'm a huge believer in making crafts light-hearted where appropriate and there is definitely a market for items that are funny. Designs with amusing elements will appeal to people with the same sense of humor: this is particularly relevant if you are making a design with a relative or friend in mind, as you will know what makes them laugh. You may be able to bring a personal joke into the design about an event you shared together, or a nickname with a funny story behind it. All of these considerations will just help to make the design more special and the gift more unique.

Cartoons

Cartoons are a well-recognized part of modern life that can be seen in a variety of uses. From comic strips in magazines to animation, from advertisements to the art world, cartoons are used for many different purposes and can be adapted for pyrography use easily. Because of their simplified nature, they can be a very successful source of inspiration for someone who is starting out in pyrography and still building up their confidence and experience. A cartoon image, such as an animal or person, can be used in complete isolation, or you can create an entire scene that tells a story of some sort.

You can have such fun with pyrography designs. Having said that, I never thought that I would make a personalized hairbrush for a cat called Sneaky Pete…

A favorite phrase was included under the box lid to add an extra personal touch.

Cartoon designs can be very simple, yet they are so effective. This spatula was part of a commission for someone who loved mice.

STEP-BY-STEP GUIDE: MAKING A CARTOON IMAGE WITH PYROGRAPHY

Many cartoons are found in a comic strip format with several frames that tell a story. A border can recreate this effect in your pyrography designs.

Plan your cartoon design in pencil first, either by drawing freehand or tracing from other sources. This box was designed for a couple to keep the baby teeth of their dinosaur-loving son, so I used a dinosaur brushing his teeth as the illustration.

Draw the outline with a fine point, such as a blade. The grass was drawn by drawing the blade upward repeatedly in a flicking motion.

Add the dark areas of shadow with a small shading nib.

Add a mid-tone using a shading nib such as a spoon point or similar.

You can then add depth and form by using a tone that falls between the darkest areas of shadow and the mid-tone.

Finally, I added some textural details using a circle stamper to give the effect of scales on the dinosaur's body.

Caricatures

Caricatures are usually portraits of a cartoon nature that exaggerate key features of someone's physical appearance. Creating a good caricature is a true talent, as the success of the image depends on whether the viewer is able to recognize who is being portrayed. A friend of mine is a graphic designer who is extremely good at illustration, especially capturing the personality of people in detailed caricatures. I've translated some of his illustrations into pyrography designs with great success.

If you want to try and create your own caricatures for your craft designs, carry out your research by gathering plenty of photographs of your intended subject in a range of situations. Think about the personality of the subject, and look at their key physical features. A caricature works by emphasizing these characteristics in an exaggerated manner, so start to focus on this while you sketch. If someone has a big nose or ears, then these will become even more prominent in a caricature. If they are very tall, perhaps you may want to incorporate something alongside them to portray this in an overstated manner. You may draw them towering over a skyscraper or another large object. Consider the manner of the person as well. If the person is renowned for their serious mood, then make sure their expression emphasizes that and consider creating a scene that should test their sense of humor!

I used the caricature design of my daughter to create a little door hanger for her bedroom.

Many humorous images are often accompanied by a caption or quote to complete the joke. This text may form a play on words or pun relating to the content of the image. It can be in the form of a separate caption alongside the image, or it may be incorporated as part of the image itself in the form of a speech bubble. If you decide to use either method, you will need to ensure you plan the image and layout carefully in the initial stages to allow enough room for the text. If the lettering is cramped inside a speech bubble that is too small or squashed underneath the image, the whole effect of the design will be ruined.

The strongest feature and the first step that you will need to plan is the outline. Almost all cartoons use a strong line to mark out the forms that they depict. Because cartoon designs are usually simplified and bold, they make ideal subjects for pyrography. Once you have drawn out the image onto the wooden surface, use

Caricatures make great gifts, and it is a real talent to be able to capture someone's character in such a way. This family caricature was designed for me by a graphic designer friend, Chailey Illman.

Fabric crafts

There are many ways items decorated with pyrography can be combined with fabric or textiles. Decorated wooden frames can be used to enhance textile art or examples of cross-stitch designs. Boxes can be given fabric panels to change their appearance if required.

I made a batch of Christmas tree decorations one season, using just a batch of small wooden discs and a reel of red satin ribbon. The discs were only ¾" (2cm) in diameter, so I used my pyrography pen to decorate them with simple festive symbols such as snowmen, stars, stockings, reindeer, presents, and the like. I cut the ribbon into short lengths and looped them over. I then placed glue on the back of a pair of decorated discs, securing the ribbon between them so the ribbon could be used to hang them over the branches of the tree. The combination of the deep burgundy ribbon and the warm glow of the wood looked really good against the dark green needles of the Christmas tree.

The deep red satin ribbon and the warm wooden tones of the small discs make these Christmas decorations really stand out against the foliage of a tree.

Advice

If you are ever unsure about how a project may work when combined with another skill or craft, make contact with an expert and seek their opinion. It may be that it has already been tried before unsuccessfully, or they may be able to give you guidance on the way the process works best if known. Work closely with other crafters in collaboration. Two minds are better than one, and it may be you both gain some inspiration from working in this way. When first experimenting with using pyrography on beads, I sought help from local beaders and jewelry makers about the best ways to use them. I even sent samples to them so they could add them into a design, which helped me by giving me expert advice and hands-on technical information. Working in this way can save you a lot of wasted time, effort, materials, and money!

Working with another crafter may open your eyes to a whole new range of supplies or materials you had never considered using before. Browsing the shelves of your local art and crafts shop will have the same effect. You may be tempted to experiment with adding beads, sequins, glitter, glue, paints, papers, cards, or any other available material from the Aladdin's cave of goods on display. If you give it a go on some scrap material and it doesn't work too well, you haven't lost anything from the experience.

Modern Surfaces

Pyrography does not have to be limited to traditional wooden objects. Though you can purchase an assortment of craft blanks from art suppliers, you may also wish to create items that are more unique and individual as your creative style and desire to express yourself develops. Any wooden surface that has not been treated with a varnish or other similar substance can be viewed as a potential canvas for your designs, so do not feel you are restricted solely to items sold as blanks for crafting purposes.

Guitars

For example, one wooden object that has always fascinated me from my teenage years is the electric guitar. As someone who has always loved rock music, there is something extremely iconic about the rock star wielding a stylish guitar on stage. Many guitars are highly decorative and ornate in their own right, usually due to the high quality of painted design or lacquer that is applied. Guitars are primarily wooden, so the use of pyrography is ideally suited, but rarely used. I could literally spend my whole life purchasing wooden guitar bodies and decorating them, but, unfortunately the cost would put an end to that quite quickly! Many musicians like to play instruments that are personalized to express their own character or musical preferences, so keep your ear to the ground for any aspiring rock stars who might like to own a unique guitar decorated to their own specifications.

Decorating a guitar can prove a challenging prospect. The shape of the guitar body is unlike almost any other canvas, and your design will need to be planned carefully so it works with the form rather than against it. Remember to bear in mind that other items will be fixed to the surface when the guitar is assembled: the main consideration would be the scratchplate, which can cover a large area of the guitar's front face. If you mark up where the scratchplate and other features will be located once attached, you won't waste time working on a design that will be partly hidden. As with many other items, the guitar body can be treated as a three-dimensional surface. Your design can flow over the sides and onto the reverse of the guitar body if you wish, rather than sitting on one face only as a purely flat image.

Many guitars are made of maple, ash, or alder, and are often manufactured so the stunning natural figure of the wood can be seen. If you browse on the Internet, you can find many suppliers of D.I.Y. electric guitar body kits, sold as complete packages with all of the relevant accessories and features to make a fully functioning guitar.

The unique form of the electric guitar is instantly recognizable by millions, and a blank wooden body represents the ultimate challenge to any aspiring (and music-loving) pyrographer!

The structure of the dragon design was carefully composed so that it worked around the curved form of the guitar body and the scratchplate.

The finished design looked really eye-catching and is ready to have the other components fitted in order to construct a fully operational electric guitar.

Furniture

Wooden items of furniture are very tempting to a keen pyrographer! A large wooden chair or table just has so much blank wood that cries out to be decorated with beautifully intricate designs. You may decide you would like to customize a table top so it features a games board or the names of the people who regularly sit at the table to eat. Solid wood doors are another example of an item that I often can't help but imagine what decorations I could burn into it. If you do wish to try decorating items of furniture, you will need to check first that the wooden surface hasn't been treated with any oil or varnish that may give off fumes when burned. Many craft suppliers sell small items of furniture in kit form, which are made specifically for decoration by painting or pyrography, such as three- or four-legged stools.

If possible, it is best to work on some items before they are put together: this can make it a lot easier to handle as you try to work on it with a hot pyrography pen. It can be very difficult to burn a design onto the leg of a chair once it is assembled due to the awkward shape it then has. While the components are still dismantled, it is far easier to plan your decoration and trace or draw the design onto each individual surface. If your design is planned so that it flows seamlessly across several components, you may need to leave a small section around each join blank until the item is assembled so that you can ensure the lines match up accordingly. Remember to allow for parts of the components that go inside or pass through other sections. It would be frustrating to cover up a section of the design due to a small oversight in the planning stages.

Modern and Alternative Inspiration

The modern world is always changing, with new trends, fashions, styles, and experiences developing at an astounding pace. With a little thought and planning, such developments can be adapted for use in crafts such as pyrography in order to expand the boundaries of what is usually expected. Just because a craft has traditions and a history of what has been done before does not mean the limits cannot be pushed and tested with experimentation.

The world of media and advertising has opened up an array of new creative arenas. Advertising bombards us every day of our lives through radio, television, billboards, the Internet, newspapers, magazines, and more. Logos are designed to be easily recognizable and cause us to recall the products associated with them. Certain styles of lettering are also inextricably linked to a specific brand or advertising campaign. Any or all of these factors may provide you with an avenue you wish to incorporate or adapt for use in your own design work. The world of advertising has been used as inspiration in artistic works before, such as the creations of Andy Warhol and other exponents of the Pop Art movement. Applying a modern sheen to a traditional craft may create some exciting and unexpected results, so feel free to experiment and explore any ideas that you have.

This paperweight was designed by Chris Fox, a woodturner who I collaborate with on a regular basis. It is made to the exact dimensions of a regular can and the decoration was a cheeky homage to the soft drinks industry.

Local interest

The area in which you live can be a source of potential creative inspiration. Consider what your town or community is known for: this may include landmarks, tourist attractions, history, local legend, or even a particular character trait associated with the residents of the area. If you are considering selling your crafted goods at local fairs or similar, designs based on these topics may turn out to be popular and successful in terms of sales. Many people are rightfully proud of their heritage and background, and a unique handmade design can make a perfect gift or purchase to demonstrate that.

You may wish to look into any symbols used locally to represent your town or community. Many towns and villages in the United Kingdom have a heraldic crest, which can be incorporated into a commemorative design such as a plate or shield. Local groups and clubs may also have symbols and logos associated with them that give you an idea for a new creation.

I live in the county of Wiltshire, which is renowned for Neolithic sites such as Stonehenge and Avebury. Visitors from around the world travel to visit sites like these due to their interest in their origins and construction. As a result, the standing stones are a strong symbol of the early periods of our evolution. The imagery associated with such prehistoric sites provides a wealth of inspiration for me as a craftsperson. Sites such as these are always inextricably linked with druidry, paganism, and other natural powers, each of which brings their own imagery and symbols with them. I have always been fascinated with the ideas of myths and magic since I was a child, and the associated symbols are a joy to work with.

Local myths and legends are a fantastic source of reference for your creative ideas. For example, the legend of the moonrakers is a common Wiltshire tale and has become a nickname for residents of the county. The story describes a group of smugglers, who were moving their illicit supply of alcohol in barrels, when they were disturbed by a group of Excise men who demanded to know what they were doing. The smugglers had hidden the barrels in a pond and were standing in the water holding rakes, which they moved around in the water to create ripples to disguise the hidden kegs. Legend has it that the reflection of the full moon could be seen on the water's surface, so the smugglers claimed they were trying to rake for the large round cheese they could see in the water. The Excise men left the men to their activities, simply dismissing them as mad or stupid. The images that can be created for legends such as these can result in some fantastic designs.

A more recent phenomenon in the Wiltshire area over the last few decades has been the mysterious appearance of crop circles during the summer months. Whether they are the result of unusual weather conditions, unknown natural powers, beings from outer space, or an elaborate hoax, there is no denying that the fantastic patterns are truly stunning to look at. Such forms are also ideal sources of inspiration for your craft designs, due to their strong geometric patterns and dynamic appeal.

Each geographical area or community will have its own tale to tell, and you can play your part in continuing the story through your own creations. Keep your eyes open as you travel around and try to visit any local museums or exhibitions to find out more about the heritage of where you live: you may open up a whole new avenue of creativity through looking into the past, present, and future of your hometown.

The natural forms created by the spalting in this plate reminded me of clouds, so I used this to my advantage when creating a plate based on the legend of the Wiltshire Moonrakers.

Art

The art world is an immensely diverse field to explore, and is an area that is often viewed as being entirely separate from crafts. With the limits constantly being tested by creative people on both sides of the fence, the opportunities to explore and use the ideas from other styles in your own craftwork is too good to miss.

Every artist has their own style and every art movement has its own characteristics. Many artists and craftspeople create works in the style of work that has gone before them, using the characteristics of others to inspire their own creativity. You may wish to work on a pyrography tribute to your favorite artist or movement. A favorite painting may act as the inspiration for you to create your own work in the style of the original, whether it is Cubist, Impressionist, Art Nouveau, Pop Art, or any other movement. You will be able to test your pyrography skills in translating the feel of a particular artistic style onto a wooden surface using the marks that your pyrography pen can make.

Graffiti

Art is always evolving and developing, and there are many modern styles that may inspire you in your craftwork and designs. Graffiti was once seen as the result of vandals causing criminal damage, but it has also progressed in itself to become a recognized art form. Graffiti can be viewed as an alien decoration that is out of place on the surface to which it has been applied, or it can be used in a very ingenious way that reflects the surrounding features and landscape. In the same way, you may be able to use modern motifs reminiscent of graffiti in your pyrography, which can either clash or harmonize with the surface that you are decorating.

Banksy is possibly the most well-known graffiti artist of this generation. His subversive and satirical designs use the medium of graffiti to comment on modern culture. There are many parallels in my mind between the use of a spray can and the pyrography machine. Both alter a surface that was clear or pure before the artist started, and a great deal of effort would be required to remove all traces of their work. Pyrography designs do not have to be purely placid decoration. You can use your designs to make bold statements and create your own platform of visual expression. The success of such designs is often based on the juxtaposition of two wildly different images, or the use of recognizable images in an unusual or jarring situation to provide a dramatic contrast.

If you decide to recreate the feel of graffiti in your pyrography work, the main feature is the use of strong silhouettes to give the appearance of stencilled designs. Creating clear and defined outlines is essential, along with appropriate shading to fill in large areas of even tone. You could experiment with using pointillism (stippled or dotted marks) with a fine nib on your pen to reproduce the misted effect that spray cans create. You may also wish to experiment with adding colors to bold designs inspired by graffiti.

I used an old piece of pine to make this plaque in the style of the graffiti artist, Banksy. I used the pyrography pen in a very loose manner to try and mimic the effect of a design constructed with a stencil and spray paint.

Tattoos

Another area I have been keen to explore and translate into my pyrography is the inspiration of modern tattoo designs. As I described in my introduction to this book, there are a lot of similarities in my mind between the work of a tattoo artist and a pyrographer. The scope of tattoo designs can be explored in books, magazines, and on the Internet, providing another massive resource for artists and craftspeople to refer to for visual stimulation.

One popular style of modern tattoo design is the tribal pattern. These designs are characterized by the use of overlapping lines and bands (similar to Celtic knotwork), which are combined with sharp points and shapes. They are very bold and have a strong visual impact, whether they consist of elegant narrow lines or solid areas of large organic shapes.

The use of tribal designs can easily be transferred from the human body to wooden items with pyrography. The shape and form of the tribal tattoo are often applied sensitively so they enhance and reflect their position on the human body. A delicate spike may follow the natural curve of a muscle, or a larger area of the design may mirror the shape of a shoulder blade. The same technique and deliberation can be applied to the use of such designs on a wooden form or surface.

As with silhouettes and other detailed work, the preparation and application of the outline is vitally important when creating tribal patterns in pyrography. The success of the lines in each

Tribal designs such as those used in modern tattoos are a rewarding challenge to any pyrographer. The success of the design hinges on sharp points and crisp flowing lines.

pattern is reliant on their sharpness and clarity. Some parts of the pattern will have lines that are completely parallel, whereas other areas will show two lines tapering smoothly to an elegant and sharp point. The negative spaces between the lines will also need to be consistent and without error. Any flaws in the quality of the lines will be easy to spot, so you need to ensure you take care and time when creating them.

There are many other visual styles and fashions that may also provide you with inspiration for your crafts. The Gothic market is a very popular alternative area you may wish to explore, as the dark and atmospheric imagery involved can be applied to a range of objects and designs. The natural features and applications of pyrography also make it very popular for the followers of pagan beliefs, such as Wicca or druidism. Any style that features a strong use of symbols or imagery will provide possible scope for you to explore your design skills.

I decorated this wooden plate with a tribal dragon design, surrounded by a textural border. To this day, it is one of my favorite pieces, a signature design for "Wood Tattoos."

This design was based on interpretations of illustrations from druidic and bardic writings. I added it to the top of a box that was designed to hold Oracle cards.

Putting It All Together: The Design Process

This chessboard is an example of what you can do with your pyrography skills once you feel confident enough to let your creativity run wild. I was contacted by a fellow member from the UK Crafts Forum website, Peter, who asked me a very short question: "Do you make chessboards?" Suddenly, I was struck by the potential provided by working on a design for a chessboard, something I had never made before. I have always loved ornate and handcrafted examples of such items.

Requirements

Peter said he had some large chess pieces that were Oriental in style but did not have a board to complement them. Due to the size of the pieces, each square on the board would need to be 2" (50mm) across but other than that, he allowed me free rein with the design.

Peter sent me some photographs of the Chinese chess pieces. They were a deep burgundy and subtle cream in color, and the figures were carved to represent rats dressed in traditional Oriental clothing. I decided I would try to find a wood similar in color to the cream chess pieces, and I would try to incorporate the deep red color of the others into the design at a later stage using paints or inks.

Getting the board

My first step was to consider the size of the material needed. The playing area of the chessboard itself would need to be 16" (400mm) square to allow for the 8x8 grid. I wanted to add a decorative border around the edge if possible, so would need to allow around 2" (50mm) extra on each side. This meant I needed to find a piece of wood measuring in the region of 20" (500mm) square.

I started researching on the Internet to find potential suppliers. My initial thought was to use a piece of wood with a natural waney edge or two, so that the bark and natural shape of the tree was still visible. After seeking advice, I realized the large size of the board could lead to warping. I also considered using a board that had been made from separate sections of oak secured together with biscuit joints.

After a suggestion from a woodturner who has supplied me with blanks before, I looked into the option of using a special composite board. Chris suggested I could use a manmade board such as MDF as the base for a board because it does not warp. The manmade board could then be covered with a good quality wooden fascia to act as a surface for the pyrography. The whole piece

Peter sent me these photographs to show me what his chess pieces looked like. I knew that the board would need to pick up on the Oriental style, and I was fascinated by the fact that they were rat people.

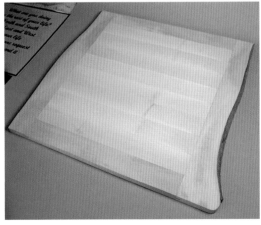

This is the special composite board that Chris made for the project. The central sycamore strips were framed with edging made of holly.

could then be framed with waney edging made from strips of local wood, glued and secured in place to help create the rustic feel. This idea sounded fascinating and Chris volunteered to make the board for me.

The board I used was made of eight 2" (50mm) strips of sycamore sandwiched and glued together to form the playing surface. It was attached to a birch plywood base for stability. This was then framed with sections made from holly, including two edges with the gorgeous waney bark edging. As soon as I received it, I couldn't wait to start burning. The surface was so soft and inviting to the touch.

Layout

The next step was to start marking the layout of the design. Half of the lines were already marked out by the joins between the strips. I measured out 2" (50mm) intervals lightly with a pencil and then drew the remaining lines at right angles to the sycamore strips. This formed the traditional 8x8 chessboard grid of 64 squares.

I started to research traditional Oriental art and decoration to provide me with inspiration for the design. I decided I wanted to decorate each black square of the chessboard with a simple motif or image. I toyed with the idea of using the design on every square. The motif would be white against the black squares, and black against the white squares to provide a decorative contrast. I eventually decided to leave the white squares blank due to the delicate figure of the sycamore, which I knew would look great when treated with a protective finish.

I selected a circular symbol that I had seen in the middle of an Oriental textile design. I chose a symbol instead of a pictorial image so that it could be viewed from any angle. I resized the image on my computer so it measured 1½" (40mm) across, printing a copy for reference to work from. I decided to draw each symbol

by hand using a pencil, ruler, and a pair of compasses. Drawing a pair of lines from opposite corners marks the center of each square. I used a pair of compasses to draw the outer circle of each symbol. I then drew a complex grid of parallel and intersecting lines as the geometric basis for each identical symbol. I also considered making a stencil, but drawing the lines with the ruler was just as easy.

I shaded the areas to be burned by lightly scribbling between the relevant lines with a pencil. This can help to prevent making any mistakes by giving you a visual reminder of where you need to burn. I would definitely recommend this if you are concerned about making a mistake. It is always better to be safe than sorry, and time spent at the preparation stages must never be considered as wasted.

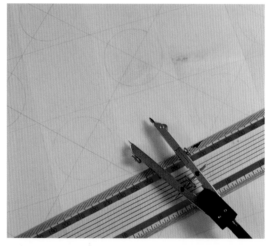

I marked the center point of each black square and drew a circle to form the outer edge of the Oriental symbol I had chosen to decorate them with.

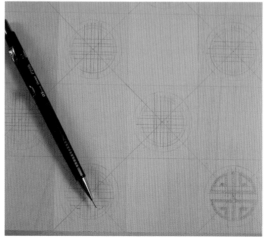

Blocking in with a pencil is a good way to indicate which areas need to be burned with the pyrography machine.

I used the edge of a spoon point nib to mark out the inner sections of each symbol and shade them.

The outer edge of each black square was marked individually, rather than a long line per row of squares, to prevent any slight overlaps. This meant that I had to draw a total of 128 lines, measuring around 21 feet (6.4m) in total!

I then carefully shaded each black square, making sure I did not go over any of the outlines I had created.

Burning the grid

When all thirty-two designs had been completed, I then used the fine edge of a spoon point nib to start filling in the central sections of each. This was a very time-consuming process that required a lot of concentration to ensure all of the lines were as neat as possible. I made a couple of mistakes where I drew lines too long: I used fine sandpaper to remove these mistakes and then drew the lines again. The most important thing is to use a nib you feel comfortable handling over a sustained period of time to make very intricate marks.

The next step was to draw the outer edge of each circular motif. I used the same spoon point nib, as the rounded edge is easy to maneuver when creating smooth round lines. You may also consider using a writing nib as they are best suited for moving across the wooden surface in a fluid motion. You may want to use a bladed nib but it can make tight curves more problematic. As the shading covers to the edge of each symbol, the quality of the line itself is not a major concern, as the main purpose is to mark the boundaries for your shading techniques. I then used the same spoon point nib on its edge to mark the edges of each black square. I drew each line carefully just inside the pencil mark so each line was slightly staggered: this ensured each square met at the very corner, rather than overlapping by a tiny amount. This may seem overly picky, but attention to detail can make or break a large design.

I then started to shade each of the thirty-two black squares one by one, creating my standard protective border along the edge of each outline with the spoon point nib first. The inner area was then blocked in using the bowl of the spoon nib in small dabbing motions to create a leathery-looking surface.

Creating the border

Once the grid was completed, I decided to create a very delicate border to frame the playing area. I measured ¹⁄₁₆" (2mm) from every outside edge of the 8x8 grid and drew a square. I then measured an additional ⅛" (3mm) from the first border lines to create the opposite edge of the border. All lines were again marked up lightly using a pencil and ruler. I used a skew blade on a medium heat to mark up the edges of the fine border, keeping the blade moving at a steady pace to create smooth straight lines. I then used a spoon point nib to shade the lines into a solid ⅛" (3mm) wide border. I left small gaps at the points in the frame in order to add some decoration at a later stage. Remember to plan ahead!

I then repeated this method to form the outer line of the border, leaving a 1¼" (30mm) frame around the playing area. I divided this into sections to create the impression and feel of Oriental panelled screens. I decided I would add decorative details inside each separate framed panel around the edges of the playing area.

At this point, I added a small Chinese symbol in the corner of the board. This was a spur of the moment decision I decided on because it looked

A framed border was completed in this way with the addition of a second line. I then broke the frame down into several sections, reminiscent of traditional Oriental panelled screens.

like an artist's signature, and also utilized the space generated by the shape of the natural edge. I used the symbol for the word "rat" to reflect the nature of the chess pieces. I added the symbol by stippling gently with a writing nib to create a mottled effect.

Border decoration

I wanted to add an elegant decoration on the sides that was in keeping with the Oriental feel of the chess pieces. I carried out research into various Oriental visual styles, looking at abstract patterns, floral designs, and much more. I then came across images of antique Japanese prints featuring drawings of samurai warriors and geisha girls. I realized I could use these as the basis for my decoration, but with a twist—I decided to reflect the rat chess pieces by using rodent features instead of human faces. I located various antique prints on the Internet and selected a male and female body. I manipulated each image using a computer program to make them the right size, then superimposed a line drawing of a rat's head on each to make them appear like "rat people". I then printed and traced each design, transferring them into the selected panels of the border frame.

I used a large skew to draw each outline of the delicate border, moving the bladed edge slowly and steadily over the surface to make a crisp line.

I added small rat outlines to the remaining corner and frame sections.

Burning the decorative accents

The outline of every panel illustration was then burned carefully using a small spear nib, enabling me to create very sharp lines with frequent changes of direction and curves.

I used a ball stylus nib to fill each rat silhouette with a solid dark tone first, which gave them a very strong visual impact despite their diminutive size. It also created a definite link between each side of the frame, and I also felt it would give the chess players something to keep their eye on as they played!

I added some delicate shading and stippling in places to create a more three-dimensional feel for the bamboo and rat people illustrations. I used a ball stylus nib so I could create a soft shading effect in small areas where other shading nibs may have been awkward to handle. I kept the shading quite simple, using a dark tone to make the image look solid in places before adding a mid tone for depth and form and to give the impression of shadow.

I created male and female rat people by combining drawings of a rodent head and traditional Oriental dress from a range of sources.

I also constructed a bamboo style design that I transferred into some of the remaining panels to continue the Oriental theme. I placed the bamboo and rat people designs into alternating panels along the outer border. I decided to fill each remaining panel with rat silhouettes in keeping with the theme. I drew a small crouching rat at each corner, and two running rats in the central panel of each side.

Each rat outline was then shaded to make striking silhouettes. These gave me the impression of rats crawling over the chessboard.

Adding color and finish

The next stage was to fill in each symbol on the black squares with a deep red ink to match the burgandy pieces. I used a narrow brush to apply the ink carefully, and allowed the first coat to dry fully before adding a second.

As the surface of a chessboard can experience a fair amount of wear when the pieces are moved across it, I used a satin varnish to protect the design on the playing surface. To ensure the red ink did not bleed into the wet varnish, I varnished the frame and white squares first, before carefully varnishing each red symbol separately. By doing so, I was using the dark burned areas as a natural barrier so the bleeding would be minimal and would not show up on the black squares. I applied three coats in total, allowing each to dry for 24 hours before the next was added.

Finishing touches

Remember those small gaps I had left in the inner ⅛" (3mm) border around the playing area? I drilled a small pilot hole with a very fine drill bit and a hand drill at each interval around the frame. I purchased some small brass upholstery studs to add a finishing touch around the playing area. I then covered the pin with a small amount of glue and pushed them carefully into each hole. This simple yet effective technique just adds a bit of interest to the design by introducing a contrasting texture and surface quality.

The chessboard was then finished and I was really pleased with the final result. This is the largest item I have ever made to date and took in the region of 30 hours of work to complete. It really was a true labor of love and it demonstrates the intricacy of design that is possible with pyrography if you want to dedicate the time and effort. The only limit to your designs is your imagination, if you are prepared to take as long as necessary to create a stunning piece of work.

I carefully added burgundy ink to the symbol inside each black square with a fine paintbrush. Two coats gave the ink a deep and warm glow.

I then inserted a brass upholstery stud into each drilled hole to add a different surface quality to the playing area.

The finished board was now ready to be sent to Peter.

Photocopy patterns at desired size.

1. Preparation

Tattoos are an extremely personal way of adorning your body and portraying an insight into your character and beliefs. Unfortunately for many people, the thought of the needle and the pain involved can put them off, as well as the fact that tattoos are permanent.

There are many ways that the style of modern tattoos can be incorporated in your work. The visual range of designs available is immense and there is something for everyone's individual taste or preferences. Decorating wooden bangles with tattoo imagery means that the decoration can still be worn and displayed on the body, but it can be changed from day to day depending on the wearer's mood and how they want to look. The designs can be as alternative or traditional as you like.

Blank wooden bracelets can be purchased in a range of different sizes, widths, and shapes from online craft supply websites if you are not able to buy them at a shop near you. The bangles can often be bought with flat, rounded, or other shaped profiles.

If necessary, prepare the surface of your wooden bangle first by rubbing it down lightly with fine sandpaper. Remove any excess dust afterward by rubbing the whole bangle with a soft cloth.

Prepare the surface if necessary by lightly rubbing it with a fine grade of sandpaper.

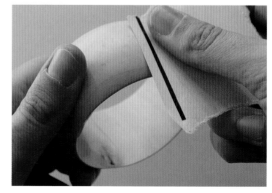

TOOLS & **MATERIALS**

- Pencil
- Tracing paper
- Eraser
- Pyrography machine
- Wooden bangle

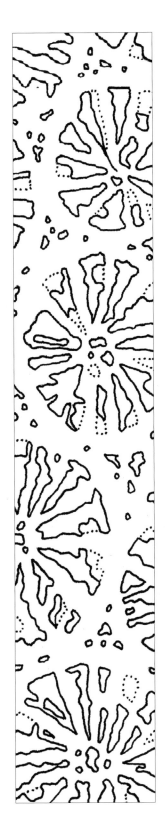

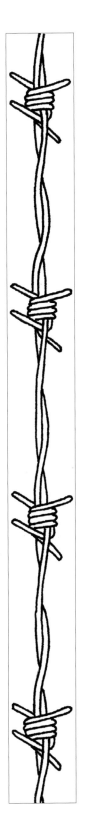

2. Plan the Design

The first consideration is to select the type of tattoo design that you would like to include on your bracelet. You can look into the type of designs available from a variety of sources, including books, websites, magazines, or even a visit to your local tattoo parlour for inspiration! There are so many different styles to choose from, including tribal, Gothic, floral, Celtic, and many more. You may wish to add some text to the bangle design, such as a name, a lyric, a quote, or a saying.

You can plan the layout of the bangle on paper first if you wish. You will need to draw a rectangle using the specific dimensions of your bangle. The rectangle will need to be equivalent to the width of the bangle in one direction, and the circumference in the other. The circumference can be worked out approximately by multiplying the diameter of the bangle by π (pi, which is roughly 3.141). So if your bangle is 1" (25mm) wide with a diameter of 2½" (65mm), the rectangle will need to measure 1" by 8" (25mm by 204mm). An alternative way of measuring the circumference is to wrap a strip of paper around the bangle and cut it to length accordingly. Planning the bangle design first can help if you are trying to create a design that flows seamlessly around the surface.

For this project, I've included four sample designs you can use to make your own decorative bracelets (see page 189). My examples include a floral design, based on primroses, against a dark background, and a textural design, based on studies of coral, both for wide bracelet blanks. I have also included a black tribal motif and a barbed wire pattern for medium bracelet blanks. Alternatively, you may find your own inspiration or creative ideas. You can then use the same principles outlined in this exercise to develop your individual creation.

3. Draw the Design

You are now ready to start drawing your design lightly onto the bangle with a pencil. If the surface is flat, you may be able to use tracing paper to carefully transfer the chosen image. If the bangle has a curved or shaped profile, it may be too fiddly to use tracing paper, so you will be better off drawing the design freehand: you can always trace small sections of the design and work your way round the bangle piece by piece, building up the image gradually as you progress. Alternatively, you can keep a drawing of your planned design in front of you for reference as you draw it freehand.

Random textural patterns are easy to draw freehand as they do not have to be exact replicas of your planned design.

Use a skew to create the sharp lines of the tribal pattern, drawing the blade lightly through the wood in a smooth motion.

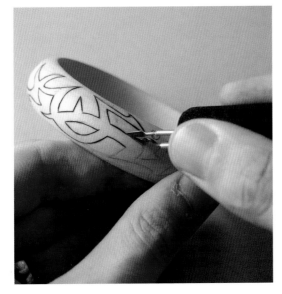

Use the skew to create the outline of the linear design for the barbed wire. Use the very tip to create the sharp curves and small lines, and the blade for the longer straight sections.

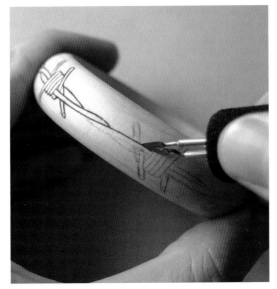

Use the tip of a spear to create the outline of each flower: changes of direction are easier than with a skew so you can create lines that are more irregular.

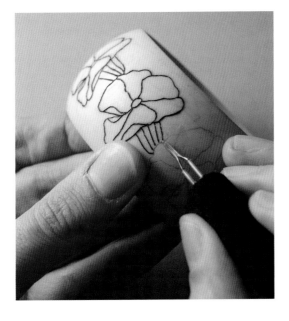

4. Burn the Outline

Once you have drawn the design onto the bangle, you can prepare your pyrography machine so you are ready to burn the outlines first. Due to the small size and unusual curved shape of the surface you will be burning on, make sure you hold the item securely and keep the hot tip as far from your fingers as possible while you are working.

I would recommend you use a fine tip to burn the outline: it is essential to keep the outlines crisp when you are working on such a small surface, because any mistakes will be obvious to the eye. I normally use a bladed nib, a small skew, or the fine edge of a shading tip such as a spoon point, depending on the quality of the lines required for each individual design. Blade tips are good for lines that are irregular and uneven, as is the tip of a spoon point nib. Skews are perfect for long flowing lines because the nib slices through the wooden surface, regardless of the grain or figure. Take time to build up the outline, working your way gradually around the surface of the bangle. When you have completed the whole design, carefully get rid of any remaining visible pencil marks using a soft eraser.

5. Burn the Detail

This step will vary, based on what your design is like.

If you want the bangle to have a strong visual impact or if the design is very bold (such as the tribal motif), then you may want to consider the use of one solid area of the same tone to contrast with the natural wooden surface. Shade the design as if it was a silhouette, using the techniques from Chapter 3 to make a successful image. Use the fine edge of the spoon point nib to shade into the sharp points of the design where two lines meet at an acute angle.

When working on a design based purely on lines, remember to use lines of different qualities to add variety and richness to the image you are creating. You can use smooth consistent lines for the outline of a drawing, but add lighter lines that are broken or irregular to shade the design and create a sense of form. The lines can be created using a fine nib such as the tip of a blade on low heat, lightly moving along the surface in one movement. It does not matter if the lines break as this actually emphasizes the effect you are trying to achieve. I used this technique to create the barbed wire design on the bangle.

For the textural design, I used a combination of effects to shade and fill the pattern. I used a range of different stippling marks to make a pitted texture across the whole bangle, using a ball stylus to create the darkest areas of shadow and a fine blade to add dotted shading that was lighter and more subtle. As your confidence grows, you may decide to create this sort of pattern completely freehand using tonal and textural marks alone with no outline, as this can create a looser and more random feel. Heavy burning for textural designs can add an extremely tactile quality to their appearance, as the pyrography marks actually change the profile of the wood rather than just decorating its surface. If you choose to use heavy texturing, fine

sandpaper can be rubbed over the finished design to smooth away any grit and take the design down a little. This adds more textural highlights between the marks of the ball point stylus.

Use the edge of the spoon point bowl to shade up to your outlines, ensuring you take care not to cross over the lines made by the skew.

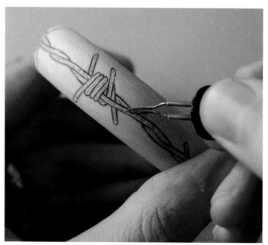

The tip of a small spear can be used to add a faint, broken shadow line, which is just enough to add some form to the delicate design.

A ball stylus nib on a high temperature can be randomly dotted over the wooden surface to create a visual and textured design, in keeping with the pitted and rough nature of coral. Use the point of a small spear nib to add small dotted details over the design.

6. Add Shading

Plan how you wish to add the shading on your floral design once you have completed the outline. I often use a dark, almost black background to emphasize the designs on bracelets. This is a particularly useful method when the design itself is quite subtle with a limited range of paler tones, such as the primrose design used here. I added only a hint of shadow to the primroses themselves using the bowl of a spoon point nib on a low temperature setting. I then added a dark shadow around the flowers with the bowl of a spoon point nib to lift the flowers and make them look more substantial. The last step is to add texture to the entire background—I find the bowl of a large spoon point nib works well to add dotted texture.

However you decide to shade the design you have chosen to create, select a nib that is the correct size for the job. Generally speaking, the size of the nib should be proportionate to the task at hand. If you are creating a fine texture or shading small areas of detail, the nib size should reflect that. If you are working on filling large areas with a tone or creating broad marks, you will save time and effort by using the largest nib that you can use comfortably and confidently.

7. Finishing

Once you have completed the shading, your design is complete. Finishing the designs with a wax treatment can give the bangles a warm and soft feel well-suited to their purpose as body adornments. Use a soft cloth to rub the wax in over the whole surface, using small circular motions to ensure the bangle is fully covered and the wax is worked in well. You can then use a dry cloth to buff the bangle and bring the item to a soft sheen. The bracelets are then ready to wear, and you may be ready to buy more bracelet blanks if you feel particularly inspired to create your own wardrobe of pyrography accessories!

The bowl of a larger spoon point nib can then be dotted over the surface to make a textured pattern.

Wooden plates and platters make ideal surfaces for pyrography. They can be found in a range of sizes and shapes. Some plates are completely flat surfaces, whereas others can be turned to feature shaped rims and edges. The individual features of the plate itself can help to inspire you when choosing an appropriate design. You may decide to add a central motif in the middle of the plate, a decorative border or band around the circumference, an abstract design across only a small section, a combination of these possibilities, or something completely different.

In this project, we will look to create a patterned border around the edge of a wooden plate. This style of decoration is popular and provides a good test of your creative skills. You need to demonstrate good control over the quality of your lines with the pyrography machine, as well as careful shading. The success of any design in a Celtic style is also heavily dependent on the time and effort that you put into drawing the rough design out in the early stages.

TOOLS & MATERIALS

- ■ Blank wooden plate of any size
- ■ Pyrography machine
- ■ Pencil
- ■ Ruler
- ■ Tracing paper
- ■ Eraser
- ■ Pair of compasses

1. Preparation

You can buy wooden plate blanks from many crafts suppliers. Alternatively, you may be able to find a woodturner who lives locally or offers a mail order service for their goods. This is particularly useful if they are willing to make plates to specified dimensions and untreated, ready for pyrography use.

I used a holly plate with a raised lip and two small grooves running around it. These grooves act as a perfect natural outline for the patterned border that will be added for this project, but it does not matter if your plate has a plain rim or no rim at all. You may find it useful to carry out some research into Celtic knotwork so you have some examples to base your design on and a better idea of what type of plate to use.

2. Draw the Outline

The next step is to draw the outline of the circular border. Draw two concentric circles about 1–1¼" (25–30mm) apart. I normally draw the circles by placing the tip of one finger against the edge of the plate and holding the pencil at the required distance from the lip—you can then draw the circle by simply rotating the plate in your hand, keeping your hand in a fixed position so the line is the same distance from the edge at all times. You can also use a pair of compasses to do this.

3. Divide the Border

The next stage is to divide your border into equal segments. You can do this by dividing it into quarters with two lines at right angles to each other. Those four quarters can then be divided equally to make eight identical segments. The border can be split into as many or as few sections as you like, as long as they are all equal in size.

Use this one-eighth of the pattern to create the full circle by repeating around the center point.

Photocopy at desired size.

4. Draw One Segment

Draw out one section of the Celtic pattern in one border segment. You can copy the example pictured in my design, or use a section of pattern from another source if you prefer. At this stage, it is not important to work out which lines go under or over to form the knots: just draw parallel tramlines. The main factor is to be certain the lines cross into the next segment at the same point on both sides, as this ensures the pattern matches correctly and flows seamlessly. Because the pattern I used was symmetrical, I drew half of the design, traced it and then flipped the paper to create the mirror image: you can see the faint pencil line of reflection that I drew onto the wood.

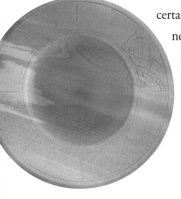

Draw the concentric rings with pencil inside the rim and divide the border into equal sections. You can then draw (freehand or by tracing) the first section of the border design.

5. Draw the Entire Border

Once you have filled one segment with the planned pattern, copy the design onto tracing paper and repeat it in every segment. Take care to make sure the lines match up at the edge of each segment. Once you have worked your way all around the border, you should have a complete and flawless pattern. This process is a very simple way to create what looks like a complicated design. The trick is to break it down into small areas and repeat them carefully.

6. Burn the Outline

You are now ready to start burning. The best way to approach the outline is to focus on burning one section accurately, which you then copy on each subsequent section. If you like, you can rub out the lines you do not intend to burn where the bands go over and under each other. With most Celtic bands, the lines will alternately go over and under the lines that they meet.

Select an appropriate nib for creating sharp outlines. For this plate, I used the edge of a spoon point, but I have also used bladed nibs.

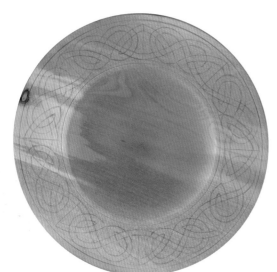

Trace the first design section and transfer it into every other segment of the border. Take care to ensure all lines match up and the design flows smoothly and seamlessly.

Use a fine nib. Make sure the lines meet and cross in the correct place. The Celtic bands should weave in and out of each other in a controlled manner.

Use the same fine nib to draw the lines of the concentric circles: these will form the edges of your border.

7. Burn the Circles

Once the outline of the knotwork pattern is finished, use the same setting and quality of line to complete the two concentric circles that form the outer edges of the border itself. Once these are finished, you can use an eraser to rub out all of the remaining pencil lines, as they are no longer required.

Use the edge of a small spoon point nib or similar to block in the smallest areas of the background, taking care to shade any acute points very carefully.

8. Shade the Fine Parts

You are now ready to start blocking in the background of the border. Some of the areas around the knotwork are very small with fine points. These are not suitable for covering with a shading point and require a great deal of care so you do not ruin the outlines you have created. Start by turning the pyrography machine to a medium-high setting. The nib should have no more than a slightly dull red glow or the setting is too high. Use the writer or the edge of a spoon point nib to carefully shade all of the smallest border sections to a dark tone.

Use the bowl of the spoon point nib to create a protective border in the larger areas to be shaded. Make sure you do not cross over the crisp outlines you have constructed.

9. Shade the Edges of the Border

Once the smallest sections are shaded, you are ready to move onto the remaining large sections. Keep the machine at the same medium-high setting but use the bowl of a spoon point nib, or a small shading nib. Start by working your way around the edge of each area to be shaded carefully so the outlines are not crossed or compromised.

10. Block-shade the Border

When you have shaded the edge of all the remaining areas, you can now block-shade the middle of each to complete the dark tones. The shaded edging acts as a protective area, which allows you to use a broader shading nib or a slightly higher temperature without the risk of ruining or distorting the outlines. You can now finish the shading in each area so the black background for the knotwork is complete.

Block in the remaining areas of tone with the bowl of a spoon point or similar shading nib.

11. Add Shadows

Turn your machine off and allow the nib to cool. You will need a nib suitable for detailed work now, to start adding some shadow to the bands. The nib you used to complete the outlines is ideal. The aim is to add a small bit of shading at either side of the points where two bands cross—this helps emphasize the effect of one band passing under the other. Set the nib to a low-medium setting and add a series of small lines that run away from the overlapping band. Place the nib down lightly and then move it away in a light flicking motion: this should give you a line which starts with a dark point but fades away. Work your way around the whole design, adding shade at every point where two lines cross.

Carefully add some delicate shading to emphasize the areas where the bands overlap and cross.

12. Add Irregular Line

The final touch I have added is an irregular line around one edge of each band. Use a medium setting and just lightly run the nib around one edge: the line does not have to be smooth or solid because it is acting as a form of subtle shading. This helps to give the impression the bands are slightly more three-dimensional and substantial, rather than a mere flat pattern. The plate is now complete and ready to be displayed. The same principle can be applied to any Celtic knotwork pattern you use in your designs, whether simple or complicated.

Add some delicate broken lines with a fine nib to add a sense of form and substance to the bands.

Appendix A
Wood for Pyrography

There are many different types of wood and they all have their own different qualities and drawbacks. Darker woods are generally not suitable for pyrography as there is little contrast available with the burned marks. The figure and grain in some woods can make them difficult to burn even or consistent marks on.

This appendix provides basic information about the most commonly available and suitable wood for pyrography, with some details about their qualities, benefits, and problems. There are numerous other more exotic woods available that may provide you with the effect or finish that you are looking for.

Alder
Color: Orange/brown.
Grain/Figure: Straight with a fine texture.
Qualities: Relatively soft. Easy to burn.

Aspen
Color: Light/pale.
Grain/Figure: Fine and even.
Qualities: Soft. Easy to burn.

Basswood/lime
Color: Light/pale/cream.
Grain/Figure: Straight with a fine texture.
Qualities: Soft. Very popular pyrography wood.

Beech
Color: Cream/pale brown/pink to red/bronze/brown.
Grain/Figure: Straight with a fine and smooth texture.
Qualities: Popular pyrography wood.

Birch
Color: Cream.
Grain/Figure: Fine and even.
Qualities: Often used to face plywood. Good for pyrography use.

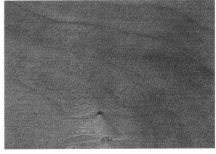

Cherry
Color: Pinkish hue to red/brown.
Grain/Figure: Straight with a fine texture.
Qualities: Good hardwood for pyrography use.

Holly
Color: Very light/pale/white.
Grain/Figure: Little/irregular with an even texture.
Qualities: Good contrast for pyrography use.

Horse Chestnut
Color: White/light/pale yellow.
Grain/Figure: Wavy or cross-grained with a smooth texture.
Qualities: Interesting surface patterns and sheen.

Jelutong
Color: Light/pale.
Grain/Figure: Plain with an even texture.
Qualities: Soft and easy to burn. Provides good contrast for pyrography.

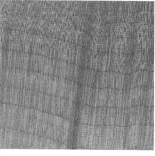

Maple
Color: Cream/pale brown/pink/ brown/red.
Grain/Figure: Even and fine.
Qualities: Good hardwood for pyrography use.

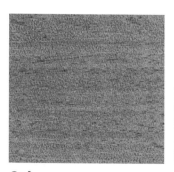

Oak
Color: Pale/light brown/red/brown.
Grain/Figure: Coarse texture. Usually straight but can be wavy or cross-grained.
Qualities: Not always suitable for complex pyrography designs due to the texture/grain. Can be difficult to burn evenly.

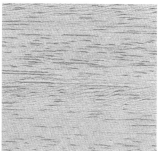

Obeche
Color: Pale/cream/yellow.
Grain/Figure: Even and striped. Fairly coarse texture.
Qualities: Soft. Easy to burn.

Pear
Color: Pale/yellow through to pink/brown.
Grain/Figure: Grain can be irregular. Fine and even texture.
Qualities: Good hardwood for pyrography use.

Pine
Color: White/straw/yellow/orange/ reddish-brown.
Grain/Figure: Straight with an even to coarse texture.
Qualities: Soft wood. Not always suitable for complex pyrography designs due to the sap, texture, and grain. Can be difficult to burn evenly.

Sycamore
Color: Pale/cream/yellow.
Grain/Figure: Usually straight with a fine texture.
Qualities: Popular hardwood for pyrography use.

West Indian Satinwood
Color: Cream/gold/yellow.
Grain/Figure: Grain varies between straight and irregular/wavy. Even texture.
Qualities: Beautiful surface provides good contrast for pyrography.

Yellow cedar
Color: Pale/yellow.
Grain/Figure: Straight grain with an even texture.
Qualities: Provides good contrast for pyrography.

Yew
Color: Orange/brown.
Grain/Figure: Irregular.
Qualities: Not always suitable for complex pyrography designs due to the sap and texture/grain.

Appendix B
Texture & Pattern Samples

During my Art & Design studies, I explored the possibilities of different textures and patterns. As well as creating my own design ideas, I looked at a range of sources to find inspiration wherever it was available. I looked at natural objects closely to discover their qualities and textural appearance, recording the results by drawing them. I worked with only a black marker pen and gradually built up a number of sketchbooks featuring hundreds of visual studies and ideas. I have gone on to use many as the basis for my pyrography designs. This appendix features a selection of these patterns, which may inspire you to find your own ideas by looking at the objects around you through more inquisitive eyes.

Many of the designs are similar but show slight changes or amendments. This shows where I explored a theme or idea to see how many different results I could develop. This is a good way to work because it allows you to fully investigate a design you feel has potential in as many ways as possible. I hope the examples here also show the wide and varied range of sources that provided me with inspiration, and help to encourage you as you create your own pyrography designs.

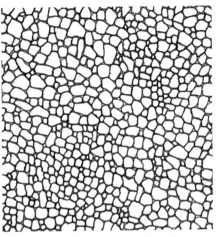

This was a simple line drawing based on a moulded glass window panel, which reminded me of a pebble beach.

I created this three-dimensional grid effect using only three different tones, creating the impression of shadows and highlights.

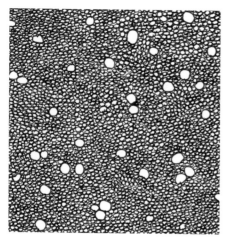

This pattern was based on the impression I had gotten from looking at a picture of lizard scales, mostly uniform in size but with the odd larger scale.

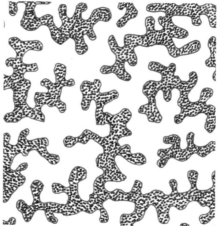

This texture was the result of some drawing experiments with curvy lines. It reminds me of something organic growing and spreading.

This pattern was created using only a pen and a circular stencil. I started with the largest circles in rows, and filled them with circles which gradually decreased in size.

I repeated the previous pattern but filled in the gaps between each circle, then colored every other circle to create a receding tunnel pattern.

This pattern is the exact visual opposite of the last. What was colored black is now white and vice versa, showing the different effects possible with minor changes.

This pattern was created using a pen and ruler. I started with a loose pencil pattern of random shapes, and then added a radiating star in each before rubbing the pencil out.

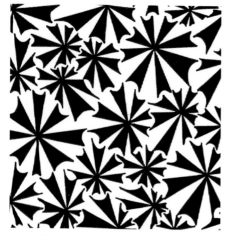

I copied the previous pattern but started to join the radiating lines together to make a more solid shaded design. It now makes me think of lots of umbrellas held closely together.

I copied the last pattern but filled in the gaps between the radiating patterns that I drew, giving a different impression entirely as the design is bolder.

Rows of circles filled with lines radiating from a different random point each time.

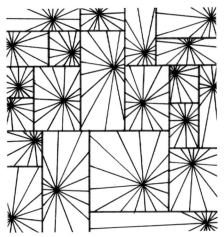

A design of interlocking squares and rectangles, filled again with lines radiating from a single point.

This was a copy of the previous pattern, but using shade to fill in an assortment of the shapes.

I saw a "THIS WAY UP" arrow on the side of a box and experimented with fitting it together in repeated rows.

This pattern was based on an image I had seen in a scientific textbook, demonstrating the way that a mold grew in a petri dish.

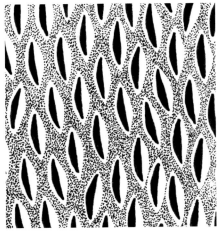

This pattern was based on the pips that you can see on the surface of a strawberry.

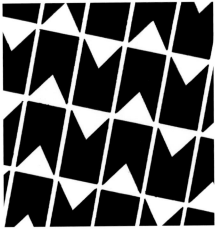

This pattern, created using a repeated black motif, unexpectedly created a pleasing visual illusion of zig-zags running over the top of the formal grid.

This pattern was based on studying the patterns of brushes being dragged through wet paint in different directions.

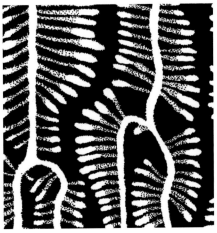

This pattern was based on a photograph I saw of intricate tunnel networks made by spruce bark beetles.

This pattern was inspired by the magnification (x60) of natural crystal formations in Vitamin C.

Resources

Wood Tattoos
www.woodtattoos.com
Pyrography craft & design by Simon Easton

www.flickr.com/photos/woodtattoos
Photostream of my most recent designs.

www.facebook.com/woodtattoos
Become a Facebook Fan of Wood Tattoos

Websites of Interest

www.craftjuice.com
Site for popular and new craft designs.

www.craftsforum.co.uk
UK-based crafts community forum.

www.cuteable.com
Treasure trove of handmade crafts.

www.etsy.com
Your place to buy and sell all things handmade.

www.indiequarter.com
Blog about designers, makers, artists & crafters.

www.onetree.org.uk
Website for the 2001 'Onetree' project.

www.ukcfis.co.uk
UK craft fair information service directory.

Pyrography Equipment & Supplies

www.craft-supplies.co.uk
Home of Janik pyrography supplies.

www.craftshapes.co.uk
Family-run business supplying wooden blanks.

www.dalescraft.com
Fine quality wooden craft blanks.

www.diybangles.com
Suppliers of unfinished wood bangle bracelets

www.dremel.com
Manufacturers of rotary power tools that can be
used in conjunction with pyrography.

www.fredaldous.co.uk
Superb range of art and craft supplies.

www.peterchild.co.uk
Pyrography & woodworking supplies store.

www.splattart.co.uk
Bespoke wooden picture frames.

www.woodworkscraftsupplies.co.uk
Supplier of wooden craft blanks, parts
and equipment.

Other Crafters Who Have Supported this Project

www.aviyaglass.com
Handcrafted glass art & jewelry by Terry Wren.

www.bodrighy.co.uk
Home of woodturner, Pete M-Jury.

www.dizatiaras.co.uk
Handmade tiaras and jewelry by Diana Hunter.

www.poisonedapplejewellery.co.uk
Jewelry designs where old meets new,
by Clare Byfield.

www.rafflesbizarre.co.uk
Handmade alternative jewelry by Jess Heath.

www.scorchpyro.co.uk
Home of fellow pyrographer, Tracey Annison.

www.suewalters.com
Website for Australian pyro artist, Sue Walters.

www.tiptoptoppers.co.uk
Handcrafted embellishments for card making
and scrapbooking by Ruth Cunliffe.

www.works-in-wood.co.uk
Home of turner and woodworker, Chris Fox.

Acknowledgments

All Photographs/Illustrations Courtesy of:

Simon Easton, Jane Easton, Harry Swain, Chailey Illman, Peter Sewell, Ruth Cunliffe, Lynsey Searle, Clare Byfield, Jess Heath, Diana Hunter, Amy Lowson, Terry Wren, and the good people at Razertip.

With Thanks

First, foremost and above all else: to my gorgeous Jane, plus Bethan, Howell, Harry, and Freddie. Also to Peggy & Gilbert Mills, Molly & Ted Elliott, Chailey & Anna Illman, Cam Merkle at Razertip, Peg Couch & Kerri Landis at Fox Chapel, Geoff Smith, Gary Beck, Graham Taylor, Al Lloyd, Barry Walker, Tim Emery, Andy Tomlinson, Perran Bateman, Matt Allen, Julie Hamilton, Andy Ward, Marc Robinson, Sue Nix, Teresa Kiely, Paul "Dave" Tuttle, Viv Joyce, Steve Pengilly, Steven Innes, Des Buckley, Ian Pearse, Jason Murphy, Michelle Norman, Nigel Woodall, Rhys Miles, Matt Hunt, Adrian Lewis, Leanne Manley, Kev & Sian Betteridge, Jim & Karen Shaw, Andy Woods, Karen Greenfield, Debbie Ashford, Ray Farrow, Alexandra Marshall, Natalie Cox, Dawn O'Rourke, Paul South, Rachel Sennett, Marian Midgley, David Frost (my tutor at MMU), Chris Fox, Pete M-Jury, Gabriel Homer, Peter Sewell, Karen Clark, Janette Crompton-Rooks, Lisa Fleming, Ruth Cunliffe, Lynsey Searle, Clare Byfield, Jess Heath, Diana Hunter, Terry Wren, Lindsey White, Graham Swan, Tracey Annison, Steve Jardine at Craftshapes, Niall O'Meara at Fred Aldous, Colin Ellis at Dalescraft, Colin Carlson at Woodworks Craft Supplies, John at UKCFIS, anyone who has purchased a Wood Tattoos design, plus all the other hard-working people out there dedicated to their crafts and the traditions of the past.

ACQUISITION EDITOR: Peg Couch
COPY EDITOR: Paul Hambke
CREATIVE DIRECTION: Troy Thorne
DESIGNER: Lindsay Hess
EDITOR: Kerri Landis
EDITORIAL ASSISTANT: Liz Norris
PROOFREADER: Lynda Jo Runkle
INDEXER: Jay Kreider

Index

More Great Project Books from Fox Chapel Publishing

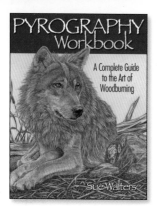

Pyrography Workbook
A Complete Guide to the Art of Woodburning
By Sue Walters

A best-seller! Renowned pyrographer, Sue Walters, teaches you everything you need to know to create stunning pyrography artwork with three step-by-step projects, and original patterns.

ISBN: 978-1-56523-258-7
$19.95 • 144 Pages

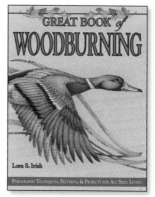

Great Book of Woodburning
Pyrography Techniques, Patterns & Projects for All Skill Levels
By Lora S. Irish

Renowned artist Lora S. Irish shares her secrets for creating stunning pyrography with techniques, patterns, and easy-to-follow projects.

ISBN: 978-1-56523-287-7
$22.95 • 200 Pages

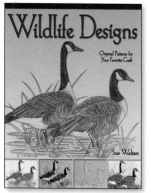

Wildlife Designs
Original Patterns for Your Favorite Craft
By Sue Walters

Whether you are a novice or an experienced artisan, these 30 designs and 10 border designs will guide you in creating images of North American wildlife.

ISBN: 978-1-56523-295-2
$14.95 • 112 Pages

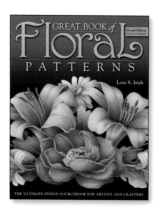

Great Book of Floral Patterns, 2nd Edition
The Ultimate Design Sourcebook for Artists and Crafters
By Lora S. Irish

More than 100 stunning floral patterns to adorn your next project. Includes a guide to identify floral shapes and create realistic shading.

ISBN: 978-1-56523-447-5
$24.95 • 216 Pages

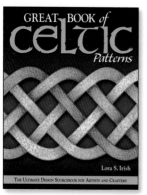

Great Book of Celtic Patterns
The Ultimate Design Sourcebook for Artists and Crafters
By Lora S. Irish

Unravel the secrets to creating knotwork as you adorn your projects with beautiful twists, braids, and textures. An essential Celtic design reference featuring 200 original patterns.

ISBN: 978-1-56523-314-0
$22.95 • 200 Pages

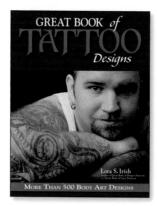

Great Book of Tattoo Designs
More Than 500 Body Art Designs
By Lora S. Irish

A great design reference for both tattoo artists and pyrographers. Artwork themes include fantasy, floral, wildlife, tribal symbols, and more—over 500 featured designs.

ISBN: 978-1-56523-332-4
$16.95 • 504 Pages

WOODCARVING ILLUSTRATED   SCROLLSAW Woodworking & Crafts

In addition to being a leading source of woodworking books and DVDs, Fox Chapel also publishes two premiere magazines. Released quarterly, each delivers premium projects, expert tips and techniques from today's finest woodworking artists, and in-depth information about the latest tools, equipment, and materials.

Subscribe Today!
Woodcarving Illustrated: **888-506-6630**
Scroll Saw Woodworking & Crafts: **888-840-8590**
www.FoxChapelPublishing.com